Country French Kitchens

# Country French Kitchens

CAROLINA FERNANDEZ

WITH PHOTOGRAPHY BY
JOHN AND CASSIDY OLSON

Gibbs Smith, Publisher
TO ENRICH AND INSPIRE HUMANKIND
Salt Lake City | Charleston | Santa Fe | Santa Barbara

First Edition
12 11 10 09 08        5 4 3 2 1

Text © 2008 Carolina Fernandez
Photographs © 2008 John and Cassidy Olson

Published by
Gibbs Smith, Publisher
P.O. Box 667
Layton, Utah 84041

Orders: 1.800.835.4993
www.gibbs-smith.com

Designed by Debra McQuiston
Printed and bound in China

Library of Congress Cataloging-in-Publication Data

Fernandez, Carolina, 1957-
    Country French kitchens / Carolina Fernandez ; with
photography by John and Cassidy Olson. — 1st ed.
      p. cm.
    ISBN-13: 978-1-4236-0192-0
    ISBN-10: 1-4236-0192-0
    1. Kitchens. 2.  Interior decoration—France. 3.
Decoration and ornament, Rustic—France. I. Title.

NK2117.K5F47 2008
747.7'97—dc22

                    2007029718

To Ernie,
Nick, Ben, Cristina and Victor
who bring me unspeakable joy

# ACKNOWLEDGMENTS

If my lifelong friend Leslie had not asked me to meet her in New York City one blustery January morning, this book might never have seen the light of day. For it was there, while wandering off by myself for a couple of hours, that I met Alison Einerson of Gibbs Smith, Publisher. She enthusiastically listened to my epiphany for this book and led me down a path where it could be embraced by others. So thank you, Leslie—and Marlyn, too. And thank you, Alison, for catching my vision so quickly.

I thank the wonderful folks at Gibbs Smith, Publisher, for their confidence in me. To Christopher Robbins, thank you for believing in me. To Jennifer Grillone, thank you for walking alongside me. To Lisa Anderson, thank you for polishing me. Your editorial suggestions have strengthened both me and this book.

I thank all of the generous and gracious families who opened their beautiful homes to my photographers and me. For by opening up their kitchens, they welcomed us into their hearts. To Daniel and Annette O'Brien, Pascale Lee, Michael and Tracy Byl, Alexander and Meagan Julian, Michael and Emily Feinberg, Susan Clements, Bill and Caroline Graham, Harold and Anita Rosnick, Don and Tina Sturges, Ron Sorensen and Carole Winer, Monique Shay, Rick and Lori Landgarten, Harmon and Beverly McAllister, Derek and Jamie Gottschall, Kent and Mari Dolby, Albert and Leslie Boris, Matt Gowan, Joanna Farber, Robert and Jennifer Krugel, Andy and Laura Payne, David Silvera and Marlyn Schiff, Chip and Chris Wilson, Bernard and Sarah Bouissou and others, thank you for sharing your joyful kitchens with us and with readers everywhere.

I thank the designers, builders, architects and specialists who dedicate their days to adding structure, order, and beauty to the world. To Valerie Bradshaw, Jani Caroli, Alexander and Meagan Julian, Richard and Susan Romanski, Carole Winer, Siobhan Daggett-Terenzi, Monique Shay, Robert Schwartz and Karen Williams, James Rixner, Lou Chiaia, Joyce Danko, Kimberly Petruska, C. Barry Marron, Joe Giuntz, Richard Latouf, Mari Dolby, Matt Gowan, Joanna Farber, Sharon Ranney, Alice Hayes, Andy and Laura Payne, Nick Geragi, Annette DePaepe, Denise Morocco, Marlyn Schiff, Chip and Chris Wilson, Don and Tina Sturges, Jerry Liotta, Andrea Hutter, Robert Morris, Julie Ann Stoner, Peter Cole, Rick Schappach and Jack Arnold, keep up your great work. It is admired and appreciated by those fortunate enough to encounter it.

I thank John and Cassidy Olson, my photographers, who tirelessly and cheerfully traveled throughout the Northeast with me in search of beauty. For doing your work with professionalism and enthusiasm, thank you. It has been a joyful ride!

I thank the individuals too numerous to count who have encouraged and inspired me along life's journey. Chief among them is my mom, Elizabeth Lehoczky. She remains my loudest cheerleader. "Second mom" Alyse O'Neill and "adopted dad" Don Mowat rank up there right beside her. To my many girlfriends, thank you for loving me when I was too busy to keep on top of the many details of your lives. You are the frosting on life's cupcakes.

I thank Brad, Larry and Shane for always going to bat for me.

I thank my children, Nick, Ben, Cristina and Victor, for sacrificing time that could have been spent together in order for me to write this book. They infuse more *joie de vivre* into my life than they will ever know.

I thank Ernie, the love of my life, for filling in each and every crack opened because I chose to be an author. He expands my heart and wraps me in a cocoon of strength and warmth.

I thank God for shaping me exactly the way that He did and for planting in me the energy and passion to write so that I might make a difference in this world.

Contents

As we seek to make our kitchens the most wonderful, *nurturing* room in our homes, we desire to impart *joie* through candlelit ambiance, uplifting conversation, laughter and love amongst our friends and family.

# The Appeal of Country French Style

This dining area sets a decidedly French tone. Ladder-back chairs surround a long rectangular wooden table, a feature found in Country French kitchens throughout the world. Using woven placemats instead of a tablecloth allows the beautiful wood grain to shine through. The chandelier is French-inspired.

We Americans possess an enduring fascination with French culinary arts, French design and, indeed, the French art of living. *Joie de vivre* tugs at our heartstrings and continues to pull us, inspire us and motivate us to infuse it into our own living spaces, lifestyles and families.

No singular room in the home serves all of these functions as does the kitchen. It is the heartbeat of the home, the room where roasts are basted and where hearts are repaired, where recipes are filed and where homework is checked, where bills are paid and where lunchboxes are packed. In the hustle and bustle of our workaday worlds, the kitchen serves purposes as varied and numerous as our family members' personalities . . . yet requires, from each of us, our earnest attempts at infusing *joie de vivre*—the cheerful enjoyment of life—into those human beings whose lives we are nurturing.

And few cultures do this better than the French. For the French, throughout time, have embraced this notion of enjoying life to its fullest, of infusing joy into everyday routines and into life spaces. They have long recognized the value of nurturing: with nurturing meals and nurturing conversations; with loving preparations and loving presentations. And we desire to impart this to our home, family and friends, regardless of how many miles across the pond we happen to live from *authentic* French culture.

As we seek to make our kitchens the most wonderful, nurturing room in our homes, we desire to impart *joie* not just through those things that are not really things at all: candlelit ambiance, uplifting conversation, laughter and love amongst our friends and family. We desire to impart *joie* through good design, architectural brilliance, major renovations, designer know-how—and yet we want all of those tangible things that add gravitas to the entire kitchen experience. We want the latest heavy-duty appliances, beautiful custom cabinetry, gorgeous sinks and handsome faucets. We want stone or wood floors, hand-glazed tile backsplashes and expensive copper cookware.

Indeed, kitchen remodeling jobs in the United States alone totaled $68.3 billion in 2005 and were projected to be at $80 billion in 2006. The reason? Sheer economics for one. As real estate values skyrocketed during the past decade, homeowners realized that the largest return on their investment came from a kitchen remodel. Most kitchen remodels, if they are done well, oftentimes return more than 100 percent of the homeowner's cost. We want to get the biggest bang for our buck upon resale, and so a kitchen redo is a necessary requirement for the home seller in order to simply get the house sold. In many cases, an outdated kitchen is the single largest deterrent preventing potential home buyers from getting past the initial walk-through.

Yet I suspect that there's much more going on here. As iPods and e-mail move us away from warm human contact, international travel moves us away from loved ones around the hearth and home, and business moves at the speed of thought, we yearn for human connection. For days gone by when time was suspended over lingering weeknight dinners and when conversation trumped nonstop cable television news. We want to slow down, to spend time with our families, to take much-needed respite from the frantically paced lives that most of us face squarely day to day, whether we planned it that way or not! We yearn for comfort. And no one creates comfort better than the French. Be it through crème brûlée or molten chocolate, warm baguettes with melted brie and homemade mayonnaise, or *toiles de jouy* and checks, we seek to be cradled in the cocoon we call home. And we hope that it's been infused with at least some aspect of French culture in one way or another.

## EVOKING COUNTRY FRENCH STYLE

Most of us have a vision of Country French culture and style. Whether through personal visits to the southernmost regions of France, through movies, television and other media outlets of pop culture, or through books and travelogues, we possess an innermost ideal of images evocative of this alluring, endearing style. We might envision sun-drenched lavender fields or ochre-washed limestone walls. Perhaps we see Provençal fabric covering the seat of a woven rush-bottomed ladder-back chair, hanging pot racks exposing gleaming antique copper pans, or hand-planed terra-cotta tiles lining farmhouse floors. Whatever images evoke Country French style to us, we desire to impart its simplicity and its warmth—indeed, its eternal charm—into our own living spaces.

With eight houses under my belt—and five different homes within as many years—the recognition of the kitchen as the most important room in the house, as well as its weight on the decorating, design and remodeling scale—has been an undeniable factor in my own family's housing equation. Regardless of regional differences across America, life stage, budgetary constraints or real estate values, the kitchen has always reigned supreme.

Throughout numerous house-hunting trips, the kitchen was always the room to which I made my first beeline. It was always the first to deserve redecorating budget allocation and the first deal-maker (or breaker) of any of the eight homes we've purchased in the past twenty-four years.

As the relocation and redecorating process continued throughout the years, my desire to infuse my kitchens with beauty and charm was always my driving force. I want my kitchen—regardless of the home in which I find myself—to reflect the nurturing quality that I hope to give those in my charge. The kitchen is not called the "heart of the home" for nothing!

As time went on, and children were both born and bred, international travel resumed. Trips to Europe brought visual and tactile experiences that further defined my tastes. During that journey, I became a Francophile. I desired to infuse into my kitchens the eternal qualities of beauty, comfort, charm and sensual aromas; honestly, the only style that would ultimately satisfy these longings was that of Country French. The organic colors, fabrics and textures of the rural French countryside speak to my soul. I found myself gravitating to deep yellows, sage greens and terra-cotta reds. Shortly after my husband's brief corporate assignment in Miami, where we were forced to rethink the impact that drenching rays of full sunlight have on color and on fabric and paint choices, I made yet another trip to France. Dinners there were eaten slowly and casually with friends and complete strangers alike, fresh flowers were visually embraced on every important street corner and warm chocolate croissants were indulged in at every breakfast. That trip to France, with all of its various images colliding in my mind, served as the crucible in which my percolating design ideas were officially smelt.

## THE INSPIRATION BEHIND THIS BOOK

When we discovered on our last house-hunting trip the house that would be our eighth and current home (and the one coming closest to that proverbial "dream"), I fell instantly in love when I took the first step across the threshold. Walking through the living areas, I sensed that this could be "the one," and nodded my head in approval—yet held my breath as we neared what I knew would be the most important room in the house: the kitchen.

As I walked in, my heart sank. The room, though large, was poorly designed. Cabinets were dated. Appliances were old. The refrigerator was small. There was no pantry. In short, it was dreadful. My throat developed a lump. Stomach flopped. As a visual artist, I knew there was no way I could tolerate living and working there; it was certainly not a place where *joie* could easily be infused shy of a complete, down-to-the-studs makeover. It could best be described by the sad, triumvirate "D's": dark, dreary and drab.

So I proceeded to do what I always do: research. I snapped up decorating books on the Country French style by the armloads and devoured every single page.

I read and reread, sticky-noted and dog-eared every photograph that might communicate to my builder, kitchen designer or husband the exact feeling, function and look I was trying to elicit through real live design. I communicated as best I could to the professionals (and to the ultimate budget carrier) that I wanted this room to represent the authentic look and feel of Country French—while living three thousand miles away from real live, authentic Country French homes.

Trouble was, only portions of Country French kitchens are preserved photographically in decorating books devoted to the French style. Most of these books focus primarily on living areas of the home—living rooms, bedrooms, entryways and dining rooms—and leave this most-used room to but a few pictures and scanty text and its complete design mostly up to our imaginations.

Secondly, professional American kitchen designers have a different vision of their job: they hope to create "magazine kitchens." Kitchens worth bubbly house tours and glossy community magazine feature stories that oftentimes serve more as advertisements for the designer and the products contained therein than for the lifestyle or inherent beauty derived from the room. Kitchens for real living? For raising hearts, minds, souls and healthy bodies? For those of us on a budget? Or for those of us who prefer the "undecorated" look of an authentic Country French kitchen?

This book, then, stems from part frustration, part inspiration . . . and from an abundance of *joie de vivre*! For in my own personal quest for design inspiration—and, indeed, for desiring to impart inspiration to you via this book—I have been invited into the kitchens of dozens of homeowners across the Northeast. The folks featured in this book recognize that the geography of Provence might not match that of Connecticut or New York, or that its sun-dappled lavender fields are a far cry from the snow-covered grounds that grace our horizons for half of each calendar year! Yet we desire to impart its light, its colors, its textures—indeed, its *joie de vivre*—into our own homes. We fully realize that we might not be able to completely adopt the daily marketing ritual commonly enjoyed in most parts of Europe into our frenzied American schedules, yet we seek to add a few of these rituals to our calendars whenever humanly possible. We look at the different needs of young families facing constant hustle and bustle and of those in emptier and quieter nests. And we seek refuge in the softness and warmth of what we perceive to be a Country French lifestyle.

And so I have examined architectural elements in detail. I have analyzed floor plans, studied cabinetry configurations and scrutinized appliance variations. I have run my hands over countless countertops, turned on oil-rubbed bronze and polished nickel faucets, tugged on cabinet knobs and custom drawer pulls. I have searched out the most beautiful folk art, pottery and cookware collections and have selected those owners who have chosen to make decoration around their collections central to their overall design schemes. I have interviewed certified kitchen designers, interior designers, builders and architects. I have visited kitchen and appliance showrooms, tile shops, cabinetmakers. All of this heavy lifting has been done to help you more clearly envision your space and to help your designer or builder or architect achieve the best execution possible. We have photographed authentic materials, used commonly throughout France and interpreted widely here in America, to help you understand what, exactly, defines a Country French kitchen stylistically. And finally, I have identified resources to make all of these components easily accessible to you. For reproducing an authentically Country French kitchen in America requires correct translation. And not everyone speaks this language fluently.

## My Inspiration to Help You

In order to help you best speak—and read—this wonderful language of Country French style, I have divided the material into sections as a French language teacher would divide your sentences: into easily identifiable parts. Fundamentals, like basic sentence structure, are first examined in order to guide you through those elements that are by necessity incorporated into a kitchen: appliances, cabinetry, countertops, sinks, faucets and eating areas.

Several common themes authenticate Country French kitchen design, and I'd like to make you familiar with them before you proceed to design execution. What, in fact, fundamentally separates Country French kitchens from American ones, and how can you identify those differences? Distinct design styles pervade that of Country French that do not influence other design orientations. How does one design the kitchen space so that it becomes authentically—*quintessentially*—Country French in style? Next, how does one infuse *joie de vivre* into one's kitchen? And is it really possible to translate an emotion or a complete lifestyle philosophy into one's kitchen? Why are tactile sensations so integral to Country French style? What do the French know about design and living that we tend to ignore stateside? Are there elements in texture that need to be examined for correct translation? And lastly, if collections built over one's lifetime reserve a space in one's heart, how does one preserve them in one's living spaces? Where do art and antiques fit into the design of authentic Country French kitchens?

I hope that by the way I have presented and organized these design elements, you will learn to fluently speak the language of the design style that I have come to know and love so much. I hope that through the generosity and hospitality of the wonderful families who graciously agreed to share their intimate living spaces with you, as well as through the careful planning and execution of the hard-working builders, architects and design teams chosen by them, that your fluency will enable you to understand how—and indeed, to ultimately choose—to infuse *joie de vivre* into this most important room in your home.

# THE "PEASANT ANTIQUES" FOUND IN THE NINETEENTH-CENTURY WOODBURY, CONNECTICUT, HOME OF ANTIQUES

dealer Monique Shay reflect the nurturing qualities for which French country folk are famous. Shay, who was born in the Normandy section of France, offers a home full of painted French Canadian antiques, which are also carried in her shop—housed in an antique red-painted barn directly behind her home. When native French families settled in Canada, they generally had more memories than substantive evidence of the furniture they left behind. As such, they relied on skilled cabinetmakers to reproduce similar pieces for their new homes. Often made of less expensive pine than the walnut and other native woods of France, they were painted in order to cover up the perceived poorer quality in the wood. This practical and seemingly naïve solution has become, in today's market, a delightful array of prized pieces, as we well know that the value of painted country antique furniture almost always exceeds that of antique furniture that has not received this treatment. The round table and painted bowl are antiques, while the ladder-back chairs and chandelier are faithful reproductions. The chairs retain the hand-rubbed painted finish that has earned Shay a national reputation and following. Beamed ceilings throughout the home hearken to earlier times, as does her antique copper collection, passed down from her family in France. Fresh flowers grace every table.

THE HARD-WORKING kitchen of fashion and home furnishings designer Alexander Julian and design partner and wife, Meagan, provides the quintessential setting for infusing *joie de vivre!* Possessing a passion for color, the couple used vibrant ochre and grey-blue on the walls; deep green demands attention on the enameled double 36-inch Viking ovens. The cherry table, made by master craftsman Sam Cousins, who also designed all of the cherry woodwork in the kitchen, stands extra high at 38 $1/2$ inches. Custom-designed with four long drawers on each side, it possesses a bold yet strikingly simple design, which allows Meagan, a gourmet cook and extraordinary hostess, to keep linens and other necessary items close at hand. Of particularly noteworthy design is the exposed shelving underneath the four long, similarly built drawers alongside the wall, underneath the cherry counter and glass-paned cabinetry. Here, Meagan stores large, flat serving platters.

MEAGAN JULIAN'S collection of copper pots and pans, rarely polished as she prefers the look and feel of timeworn and heavily-used materials, are *sous la main,* or at her fingertips. Utensils used every day for cooking are stored in a green-enameled pot, which matches her green-enameled professional Viking appliances. Countertops are made of slate and possess a beautifully bulldozed edge. Meagan cleans these counters with oil and waxed paper, giving them a wonderful patina. Note the open shelving on either side of the large windows and the shelf running across the entire length of the wall, on which rest the Julians' prized pottery, ceramics and crystal.

THE HOMEOWNERS IN THIS renovated Country French kitchen prefer dining at a small round table, and the intimacy and easy flow of conversation here is worth emulating. The classic French ladder-back chairs are handpainted; cushions are made of simple cotton checked fabric tied back country-style. Glass-paned door fronts are substitutes for previously paneled ones. The homeowner uses the desk area to coordinate the dizzying calendars of children's activities (*facing*). ❦ This homeowner takes pride not only in preparing nourishing meals for her husband and two young children but in presenting them beautifully as well. The *tableau* shows off everyday china from Skyros Designs. Glassware is authentic French crystal.

# A down-to-the-studs

renovation resulted in this updated kitchen, which possesses all of the bells and whistles required by today's homeowners. The home dates to 1894, and the kitchen renovation retained as much of the earliest workmanship as possible. The brick surround at the hearth serves as evidence; its stove hood was actually built into the original working fireplace. The kitchen island was custom-made to closely resemble the original oak, now found predominantly in the enormous butler's pantry. Two sinks service the kitchen: one is a classic white-porcelain, double farmhouse sink with copper faucets and is located near the range; the other is a smaller stainless steel sink situated closer to the pantry and microwave oven, both hidden behind custom cabinetry. A third faucet is the copper "pot filler" inset into the brick hearth. Although the couple desired closed cabinetry in which to store china, they opted for double plate racks for their everyday dinnerware. Of special interest is the copper backsplash set behind glass tiles. Countertops throughout are "Vecchio Fire" granite (*facing*). ❦ The renovation of this home called for custom flat-paneled cabinetry, set apart with lighted inset glass-paned fronts in which to showcase the couple's crystal collection. The book shelves in between serve a highly functional role for this gourmet cook. Note the turned supports, dentil moldings and Ogee edging on the granite counters (*right*).

THE HOMEOWNER SETS the mood for a *tête-à-tête* in her Manhattan home by lovingly setting out a fine bottle of Bordeaux, fresh figs and assorted breads and cheeses. A classic French snack, it fuels both body and spirit (*above left*). ❧ By bringing a bit of nature indoors, the homeowner adds visual interest to the small corner of her kitchen. The custom-made desk, whose latticework lends whimsy and charm, is by Mecox Gardens. The classic French ladder-back chair with rush-woven seat is from Pierre Deux (*left*). ❧ The sensuous warmth elicited by the earthy colors and textures of this kitchen wonderfully defies its Upper East Side Manhattan location. Sipping *café au lait* around the charming round table and the banquette covered in Pierre Frey fabric, one can only feel cradled in the cocoon of home. Antique chestnut beams frame the ceiling, lending a distinctly Provençal air to the room. Hand-painted walls add glorious color, depth and texture (*facing*).

*This* three-hundred-year-old home shared by antiques dealer Carole Winer and her singer-songwriter husband reflects the warmth elicited from authentic Country French style. The timbered ceiling is a quintessential design feature; in this case, it provides both structural practicality and aesthetic sensuality. The brick hearth with granite countertop is decidedly French, as are the antique pine floors, laid at forty-five-degree angles to squares of terra-cotta clay tiles. Tiled countertops, simple window treatments with cheerful Provençal fabric and the antique side table adjacent to the center island lend authenticity to the room. Note the side table's imperfect alignment, a quality the French prefer. Also of significance in imbuing warmth and French charm to the room is the vast array of French antiques, including the oval handpainted dining table, ladder-back chairs and *dressoir* filled with Winer's collection of Quimper. The chandelier and accessories throughout are French antiques similar to the eighteenth- and nineteenth-century French antiques for which she is known and which are carried in her shop, Country Loft Antiques, located in Woodbury, Connecticut.

Using her knowledge and expertise in French design acquired while living in France for a number of years, as well as through her ownership of the renowned Westport shop, Parc Monceau, homeowner Joanna Farber completely transformed her home with her vast collections of French antiques. In the dining room, Farber showcases her collection of antique French pitchers in the eighteenth-century *vaisselier,* crafted of walnut and with provenance from southern France. The dining room table was likewise crafted in France using reclaimed old walnut to reproduce an antique monastery table that Farber admired. The chairs are upholstered in fabric from Pierre Deux. In classic Country French style, they mix and match; several different fabrics are used in the set, all in complementary colorways *(above).* ❦ Enlisting the help of her builder, Farber installed antique doors directly over cut-out sections of Sheetrock and chose to use no overhead cabinetry. Wood beams were reclaimed from upstate New York; walnut doors were salvaged from France and used throughout the kitchen and dining room; butcher block was custom cut for countertops; and walls were painted a lovely ochre color. In classic French style, cups, glasses and bowls are *sous la main;* Farber installed a ledge on the U-shaped island, which is made of Sheetrock and faux-painted to resemble concrete. It holds all the glassware, bowls, cups and plates she needs to serve breakfast to her family (*facing*).

SALLE DE BAIN

• PRIVÉ •

IN THE EATING AREA OF THE KITCHEN, ATTAINED AFTER
TAKING DOWN AN ORIGINAL WALL, CLASSIC FRENCH

blues and yellows are used to brighten up the small corner of this wonderfully low-key room. The tablecloth is oil cloth, purchased in France by the homeowner. Four painted antique chairs surround the table, which boasts a hand-hooked folk art rug underneath. Note the delightful Provençal fabric at the window valance. Cookbooks fill the iron baker's rack, another quintessential Country French kitchen piece, popular for its ease in transfer from house to house—or generation to generation—as well as for its "breathability" factor (*facing*). 🍃 The homeowners of this classic cottage have such great eyes for design that they prefer to do everything themselves. The undecorated look of their home is reflected in its innate charm and timeless appeal. The husband, a professional painter, installed reclaimed cabinets he acquired from a different house; serendipitously, they fit perfectly into the

space of their own kitchen. He handpainted each one a warm buttery yellow. He also applied bead board to the ceiling and painted it a creamy white. Butcher block countertops were also installed, giving the room warmth and country charm. New appliances, as well as a new white porcelain sink and polished nickel faucet, bring the room up to date. The wife is a proficient antique collector and her beautiful eye for design is evident in the details that abound. Note her clever style of bringing the outdoors inside: an aged zinc washbasin is used in lieu of a traditional drying rack; a miniature birdbath holds an ivy topiary; a concrete garden dish holds sponges and soaps. Splashes of blue and white china infuse classic charm. Pots and pans are hung on hooks at arm's reach. Hardwood floors are covered with hand-hooked rugs, a signature design detail of the wife's that is carried throughout the home (*above*).

IN THIS WARM AND inviting kitchen, designed entirely by the homeowners, original elements dating to 1760 add distinct Country French charm. The leaded glass-fronted cabinets are original to the home; bead board on the lower cabinets was added later in a partial renovation. The arched window with wood-stained trim beautifully complements the antique exposed beams and is classic French design. The cheery yellow walls and terra-cotta floors are quintessentially Provence-style. Fleur-de-lis countertop tiles bring out the handpainted ceramic work found on accessory pieces loved by the homeowners, who travel often to France. The faience-inspired backsplash tiles play off the pottery for which the French are well-known. Fewer things have greater impact on authentic French kitchen design than do overhanging pot racks; this one does the job with panache, displaying the owner's fine collection of well-used copper. A local artist painted the farmyard animals on the kitchen island, which is set with metal chairs, seemingly brought in from the garden.

# WALNUT AND *slate floors* SERVE AS THE COLOR BACKDROP FOR THE EIGHT DIFFERENT PAINTED

finishes used in the home that designer Mari Dolby shares with her husband and two teenage children. Pulling out the warm earthy tones of southern France, Dolby utilized classic French design style by incorporating color into each of the pieces, which she commissioned local craftsmen to make and install. She knew that she wanted her kitchen to look as if it could be found in the countryside of France, and she brilliantly incorporated this spirit into every inch of the room. The L-shaped island is made of walnut, the wood most commonly used in French furniture; the Carrara marble-topped pastry table, the base of which Dolby designed, is likewise painted and juts out slightly in classic Country French misalignment style. Dolby commissioned local master carpenter Joe Giuntz to make the plate rack based on an original antique that she had seen in a design magazine; it was painted black and distressed to

look as if it had acquired age. It holds the Dolbys' collection of French china, which they acquired on a trip to Paris. Similarly, Dolby asked Giuntz to craft the blue-painted hutch, which serves as the family's appliance center. Counters are limestone. Antique hand-hewn fir beams hold a Pennsylvania provenance (*facing*). 🌱 In the adjoining breakfast room, Dolby continued the flooring with the walnut and slate grid. Note how the various colors of the slate, laid nine per square and outlined with walnut, are picked up in the warmth of the wood as well as in the ochre-painted and glazed ceiling. Radiant heat pleases the family's black lab, who frequently rests by the French doors leading to the patio and formal gardens. Full sun bathes the room in warmth; cheerful Provençal fabrics in coordinating colorways adorn French upholstered and wood-turned chairs. Note the gorgeous ironwork base of the wood-topped round dining table (*above*).

THIS LARGE KITCHEN in the Sturges home represents the best of Country French style with a decidedly upscale American twist. French elements, such as the custom-designed slate back-splash surrounding the hearth, custom-made cabinetry, gleaming wood floors and natural stone counters, all add to the French-inspired design scheme. Sturges commissioned painter Susan Grissom to striate all cabinets, which arrived from the carpenter unfinished, to give them an artistic hand-rubbed look. Using local talent and materials is a decidedly French approach to decorating one's home.

## CHAPTER TWO

Authentic Country French *style* has as its fundamental theme the notion that

ties to the past represent lines to a family's future. Pieces incorporated into one's home

need to reflect family histories, connections and stories.

# Fundamental Design Distinctions

The differences in the ways that Americans and the French approach the design of their kitchens are so distinct that it is glaring. While American homeowners desire remodeled kitchens (or kitchens in newly constructed homes) to be glossy, showy and magazine-quality picturesque, Country French kitchen designers—who are, in fact, generally the homeowners themselves—abhor the notion that homes are personal "advertising statements" or ostentatious displays of wealth.

## LET HISTORY BE OUR GUIDE

After the French Revolution, the population withdrew notions of eye-popping drama and opulence, and relied on the warmth drawn from simplicity and understatement instead. For by relying on egalitarian values for almost two centuries, the French country folk, most notably those living in rural parts of Provence and from whom we draw Country French inspiration, prefer their homes to possess similar ideals of restraint, warmth, modesty, frugality and functionality. Beauty will always play the starring role. But French houses of this southeastern Mediterranean region rarely promote themselves; indeed, even landmark houses known for their exquisite architecture, landscaping or proximity to the sea boast little of the prized possessions held inside. The notion of American super-sized (albeit oftentimes empty) Mc-Mansions is frowned upon by the French. For generations, homes across the French countryside have been modestly but genuinely constructed and decorated, with less regard for size than for quality of workmanship. Local craftsmanship is honored for strict requirements of quality; beauty, form and functionality still reign supreme in decisions regarding the home in both its exterior and its interior decoration. The functional building element of exposed timbers and beams is the perfect case in point: they serve a structural purpose, indeed, but also they hold equally important aesthetic appeal. As such, they represent quintessential Country French style.

It is not an overstatement to say that the French prize possessions for their provenance. Indeed, the idea of purchasing something new for the home without any connection to the past—to a family line or to one's heritage—is foreign to them. Authentic Country French style has as its fundamental theme the notion that ties to the past represent lines to a family's future. Pieces incorporated into one's home need to reflect family histories, connections and stories. Nearly threadbare fabric-covered chairs would hold a greater place in the home than would brand-new upholstered pieces with no sign of wear or tear. Country French style exudes evidence that families are busy living life—that they don't operate in design vacuums, yet function heartily in the daily activities of hustle-bustle life; that kitchen countertops will inevitably stain, floors will eventually crack and walls will indeed require both plaster and painting magic.

The tug of the family pulls like an umbilical cord back to places of origin, to birth homes, to churches where important ceremonies took place, and to familiar shopkeepers and artisans and *patisseries*.

It is this desire to impart meaning and warmth—indeed, history—into living spaces that fundamentally separates authentic Country French style to decidedly unique American style. If one wishes to evoke the style found in the pages of this book, a shift of mindset is required. Dispose of notions of new and contemporary and large and pretentious. Substitute, instead, the desire to impart warmth, history, beauty and French panache. Fundamentals, then, need to be examined in an effort to see how Americans can correctly *translate* these values into their own homes in general, and into their own kitchens in particular.

## KEY HISTORICAL ELEMENTS

In both early American and early French homes, the kitchen and gathering room were one and the same. This "keeping room"—*salle*—provided the space for all of one's family activities. Separate stoves did not exist for cooking. Instead, meat and fowl were roasted on a spit and grains were stirred in huge pots—*cremailleres*—over open fires in brick or stone-lined hearths. The hearth was, without a doubt, the focal point of every authentic country kitchen in both America and France. It served not only as the area to cook one's food but also as the place to heat one's home. Large troughs—*pilos*—were used for drinking and bathing, the latter being a rarely enjoyed ritual and, when done, performed with little privacy. Stone sinks—*eiguies*—were placed next to the fireplace in these large gathering room kitchens, or even in tiny lean-tos—*gatouilles*—next to this dominant room. Hand-glazed terra-cotta stones or handmade brick surrounded the hearth and covered the floor. Separate and distinct areas of this large room held places for daily functions: for eating, preparation, cleaning or gathering.

## TURNING POINTS

These basic sensibilities dominated the design and decoration of kitchens on both sides of the Atlantic for a couple hundred years. And then around the time of the 1939 World's Fair, notions of modern design were redefined. Interestingly, most American kitchen designers—unlike their French counterparts—still cling to these "rules" regardless of their appropriateness to today's lifestyles and home design configurations.

Noted kitchen designer Rob Morris freely expressed his opinions about these common design "rules." The ubiquitous "kitchen triangle," he maintains, still holds center stage in design preliminaries across America. The "rule" that the triangle between the refrigerator and sink and oven or cooktop be relatively congruent has stayed intact among American kitchen designers for several decades. Yet, because this notion originated with the introduction of the modern-day refrigerator into homes that previously only possessed an icebox, it appears to be both outdated and overused. Refrigerators, for example, designed today with over-sized widths and heights, need to find long expanses of wall space with sufficient depth to match; their proximity to the sink and cooktop is important, but it cannot always follow a precise prescriptive. French kitchen design, on the other hand, abides by common sensibilities pertaining to function; if the sink, cooktop and oven are all within a healthy working relationship to the refrigerator and to each other, then the setup works. There is no underlying rule around which to design the space.

Other American design "rules" abound. The notion that countertops need to be 36 inches high will be ever-present until appliance manufacturers change their dimensions. One must conform to some standards and specifications when designing kitchen spaces, after all. Until we change our design practice of placing our dishwashers next to our sinks, for example, or until more of us adopt the dishwasher drawer model versus the standing dishwasher model, we will be forced to conform to this height. Yet how many taller women—or taller men—prefer working at countertops of different heights or placing the dishwasher elsewhere? In authentic Country French design, these specifications would prevail only if they met requirements for pure functionality. They would be set at this height to meet function more than to conform to a "rule."

And the rule that work surfaces require a comfortable separation of 42–48 inches seems an outdated notion as well, says Morris, for it exists primarily to accommodate two people working in the kitchen at precisely the same time, hovering over each other and crossing paths in ways that are not commonly necessary. Separations can be far narrower, Morris argues, because two people do not usually need to cross over into each other's workspaces while cooking. Additionally, it is generally easier to work in "opposite work spaces" than it is to work in "adjacent work spaces." One can simply pivot back and forth between work surfaces or prep areas, such as the range or the chopping area, allowing for these separations to be narrower and for the saving of precious workspace square footage.

## Incongruities

These commonly accepted "rules" of American kitchen design, while nearly sacrosanct, are generally ignored in authentic Country French kitchen design. Because the French have different patterns of preparation and of gathering, a propensity to incorporate disparate objects into their kitchens, and because authentic Provençal kitchens are often designed by the homeowners themselves, fundamental design differences remain.

For example, a Country French kitchen might incorporate an antique table covered in marble for use in preparation for baking. Marble-topped tables remain extremely popular surfaces for bakers worldwide, as the material stays cold and allows for the easy handling of flours and dough. The height and length of the table might be completely incongruous with that of the nearby range or countertop. Yet the French will prefer it to something newly constructed and with perfect alignment, or with a surface that does not lend itself easily to the task at hand. This element, which exudes the charm for which we yearn when designing our own versions of French kitchens, is met with some disdain by modern American designers, who, for the most part, desire things to be in perfect alignment and congruity.

Likewise, an intricately carved antique armoire used to hold kitchen linens might appear to be in total design disarray when juxtaposed with a simply constructed farm table, with its straight legs and four-plank surface. Yet the French would rather place these two objects in the same room than they would perfectly proportioned, newly designed pieces lacking distinct family provenance. And few could argue that incorporating antique pieces breaks the monotony of wall-to-wall cabinetry, or that the differences in texture or patina or color yield pleasing aesthetic value to the room. Many Americans, however, have trouble with this concept and prefer all cabinetry to match perfectly and to be in the exact same design style of other wood pieces in the room.

So, too, the American predisposition for encumbering center kitchen islands with cooktops or ill-placed sinks is decidedly *not* Country French. The Country French kitchen would happily place a solid antique table with perfect functionality in the kitchen and leave it that way. It would remain an empty work surface because it is needed for just that: work. Center kitchen tables are more commonly used for rolling out dough or for lining platters with food. This follows no design "rule," existing purely for practical purposes. American kitchens, on the other hand, tend to utilize center kitchen islands for serving quick breakfasts and for washing and chopping vegetables for the dinner salad, requiring many to incorporate a sink, no matter how much it divides the workspace. And frankly, some American kitchens are so large that the omission of that extra sink would constitute foolish design. The common practice of arranging bar stools underneath island counters—indeed, using them as substitutes for dining tables and chairs—is more an American custom than a French one, too.

And speaking of work surfaces, authentic Country French kitchens always use indigenous natural materials. Soapstone, limestone and wood all find their places in countertops in Country French kitchens. They would never embrace the notion of using Corian for worktops; kitchens in southern France would rarely use the practically ubiquitous granite-topped American countertop because of its inaccessibility. For while parts of France, in particular the northwestern province of Brittany, hold huge quantities of indigenous granite, other regions do not have access to it and prefer instead to use materials native to their nearby surroundings. Homeowners in Provence would prefer using materials easily excavated from local quarries and masterfully cut by a local craftsman, or *tailleur de pierre*. Limestone, then, is one of the most commonly used stones.

Hand-glazed terra-cotta would find its way into most Country French kitchens as well, although its use would be confined more to handsome flooring or to artfully designed backsplashes. And while Americans design fancy edges for their countertops, those found in kitchens in Country French homes are usually far simpler. A fine white marble top for a table would most likely be generously cut yet simply finished; it would rarely possess a fancy Ogee edge. Native wood might cover one of the work surfaces, but it would be preserved with oil rather than protected with high-gloss polyurethane. Native soapstone might line the central farmhouse-style sink, and it would be hand-carved by a *sculpteur sur pierre,* or expert stone carver.

In choosing materials for your own kitchen, you might prefer to make the same choices as do the French in order to achieve the look most commonly associated with Country French style. However, one could easily argue that by using materials native to the United States—or to your own region of the country—you are exercising an authentically French practice. In the end, you must decide which approach feels right for you and your home. Both approaches could be considered authentic in their unique ways.

## THE DEMAND FOR INDUSTRIAL-STRENGTH APPLIANCES

On both sides of the world it is generally considered to be more authentic and more sensible, except in a few instances, to build the cooking range into the wall rather than to put it out in the middle of the floor. Hearths dating to earlier times were always built into a wall. Today's ovens and ranges serve the same purposes as did these centuries-old hearths, and while we are no longer constrained in our design in the same way that rural countrymen were hundreds of years ago, this serves as timeless wisdom for today's design principles. It is as true today as it was then: ventilation remains generally easier and more trustworthy if it is done alongside a wall rather than from an overhead vent constructed in the middle of one's room. There are exceptions to this practice, of course, but placing priority on the practical solution to ventilation is a decidedly Country French approach. And it is this focus on practicality and function, rather than on "kitchen code" or "rules," that separates the two cultures' design practices.

The current craze for stainless steel industrial-strength or professional-quality ranges and ovens is well-deserved. Kitchen designer Morris warns, "Avoid false economy!" If you are considering the purchase of an industrial-strength gas range, purchase a model with BTUs of at least 12,000–15,000. Anything less does not warrant using gas, claims Morris, and you're better off using a humble four-burner electric range. If you truly cook, you will need the extra power to hold that 12-inch skillet and to heat food quickly and efficiently.

Ovens, too, need attention in the overall design of the kitchen. The idea of possessing two ovens in one's kitchen is commonplace in America. And the range of options is wide. Modern ovens incorporate convection cooking into the traditional unit. Design specifications vary from manufacturer to manufacturer, as do quality of materials and BTUs. Electric ovens might be more preferable than those heated by gas; oftentimes it is simply the homeowner's personal preference that determines the course of action. Yet gas ovens yield juicier foods and might be a more attractive alternative for cooking meat and fowl; electric ovens produce dryer heat and are preferable for baking. Could you incorporate both into your room? These large appliances will absorb a good chunk of your remodeling dollars, so do your homework carefully.

Modern microwave ovens incorporate convection cooking in some models, although some in the trade remain wary of possible inherent design concerns: microwave ovens generally function best when the interior space is small, while convection ovens generally function best when the interior space is large, as the increased area better utilizes the continuous circulating air flow from the internal fans. Combining the two into one unit might serve as an appealing feature to many buyers because of the pure convenience factor, yet it gives others pause because of the engineering factor. Carefully study the design specifications when shopping for this appliance.

## FRILLS AND FLOURISHES

Other recent additions to the appliance market are built-in steamers; these certainly have their place and generally perform quite satisfactorily. Built-in coffee and cappuccino makers are enticing as well. But carefully consider the costs against the benefits. Will the design remain to your liking within the next ten years and will the technology remain commercially viable upon resale? Another hugely popular built-in unit is the warming drawer. Generally performing at temperatures of 70–200 degrees Fahrenheit, they provide a way to keep dinners warm amidst a family's frantic, erratic weeknight schedule. But consider whether this added convenience is worth the incremental expense: if you possess two expensive ovens and a cooktop, do you truly need another space in which to heat food? On the other hand, if you always think of the resale factor when renovating, will the absence of a warming drawer earn a design demerit?

## THE CHILL FACTOR

The other large kitchen appliances that deserve considerable attention are the refrigerator and freezer. They will garner a large portion of your design dollars and energy bill, as well as a hefty piece of your overall kitchen real estate. While Americans tend to prefer covering up refrigerators/freezers with custom wood panels or stainless steel fronts, the French admire the look of authentic antique ice chests and cover theirs accordingly, if they do so at all. One of the problems underlying our tendency to cover up these appliances is that, frankly, we have a love-hate relationship with them. We're not quite sure whether we want to hide them or expose them! If we choose to expose them, we might opt for matching stainless steel fronts; these have remained immensely popular for years, although families with young children still go half crazy with efforts at keeping messy fingerprints at bay. (No getting around that one!) A less popular American design trend—but one that is gaining some traction—is to expose the fridge/freezer by buying a glass-fronted model. But this option has two enormous strikes going against it from the start: it is an expensive alternative (try finding a superior model without practically breaking the bank; there are only two manufacturers designing glass-fronted units, both of which ride in the high-end market), and we Americans like to keep some of our living habits a secret (try convincing homeowners with teenagers that they should opt for a glass-fronted peek into their leftovers). We cannot be persuaded into thinking that the advertisements for glass-fronted fridges containing whipped-cream parfaits in perfectly-matched stemware look like our own realities!

Many of us choose to hide the fridge/freezer behind the same custom cabinetry that we have used throughout the kitchen. We desire a continuous, cohesive look, and this is the best way in which to do just that. In the end, one of the frustrations in choosing a refrigerator/freezer is simply the range of options: if you opt out of stainless steel or glass or cabinetry, you are left with a black or white or almond face, all of which have become increasingly dated stylistically. So take the time to study the appliance market carefully before making your final decision. You might wind up changing your mind several times—as I have—before settling on the best option for your family.

## THE CABINETRY CRAZE

Similar ideals of functionality and economy apply to cabinetry. Authentic Country French style generally dismisses the use of upper cabinets, preferring instead the accessibility—and creative opportunities—inherent with open shelving. The French have a natural propensity to have things in full view and within arm's reach. So shelves hold glassware and *cassoulets,* hanging plate racks hold daily dinnerware, and countertops hold buckets of utensils, measuring cups, rolling pins and flour bins.

Americans find the notion of exposing everyday kitchen objects counterintuitive. For gorgeous—and expensive—custom cabinetry needs to do its job, doesn't it? While most Americans prefer perfectly aligned, paneled custom woodwork to line both the upper and the lower spaces of their kitchens, hiding from public view the "distasteful" elements of their kitchens, the French find wide appeal in these tools and gain creative energy from artfully arranging them, as well as in finding and displaying objects of functionality and sentimentality. A happy flea market find, such as a ceramic rooster or a papier-mâché pig holding the daily menu, will settle comfortably next to a hardworking rolling pin or glass mixing bowl. Never mind the dust; the objects are used with frequency, prohibiting dust to find the time to settle! Never mind the clutter; the artistic possibilities drive the charm factor and therefore make it all forgiving!

Americans, however, possess an insatiable desire for matching upper and lower cabinetry, and we spend an inordinate amount of money acquiring it. If you prefer this look and yet seek to style a kitchen that reads *a la française,* hire a skilled, local master craftsman to construct custom cabinetry for you. Utilizing the resources of your designer, architect or builder, work with your cabinetmaker in designing woodwork to your exact specifications. Whether you prefer raised or flat panels on your cabinet doors, flush or overlaid drawers and doors, painted surfaces or beautifully waxed woods, rest assured that whatever your desired look—be it American or Provençal in aesthetic or function—this *approach* to the process is authentically Country French.

Joanna Farber's dining room is given Country French charm with exposed beams that were reclaimed from upstate New York. Natural sunlight floods the room, streaming in through the skylights. The hunt table, located underneath the window, is a nineteenth-century walnut piece from France. Of special interest in this wonderful room is Farber's adaptation for cupboards: she used reclaimed antique walnut *bibliotique* doors that she discovered on a buying trip in France and contracted her builder to fit them over cut-out sections of Sheetrock. Shelves were added so that the cupboards are not only beautiful but highly functional as well, storing Farber's collections of china and crystal. In classic Country French style, they do not match, as they are from two separate pieces. The Louis XV hinges are original to both.

THE EXPOSED BEAMS in antiques dealer Monique Shay's expansive kitchen add further cohesiveness to the room. An enormous space, the kitchen employs clever design by bringing the crisscrossing beams into play; they help direct the eye to all four corners of the room and keep its beautiful design aesthetic intact. Like other wood used throughout Shay's home, the beams are treated with her signature handpainted and hand-rubbed finishes (*left*).  These reclaimed antique chestnut beams hail from Connecticut and add enormous aesthetic appeal to this Manhattan home. Of particular interest is the design of the range hood, which incorporates the beams to perfection. Designed, plastered and handpainted to look like antique limestone, the hood is actually made of foam; the vent is hidden underneath. It represents a wonderful exploitation of modern technology in this most enchanting turn-of-the-century-styled Country French kitchen (*above*).

# The fabrics USED IN THIS WONDERFULLY LOW-KEY COUNTRY FRENCH KITCHEN COME FROM DIFFERENT

and distinct phases of the homeowners' lives. Pillows were purchased on travels; fabric at the window was purchased on impulse. With five different patterns playing off each other, the design goal had little to do with perfection and everything to do with infusing a well-lived aesthetic into this charming sitting area. The exposed beams add quintessential French flavor to the room (*facing*). 🍷 This entryway, leading to the kitchen from the front door, serves as the perfect welcome spot when reentering the cocoon of home from the hustle and bustle of everyday life. Coats are hung in the closet, which is original to this circa 1760 New England home; umbrellas are easily accessible; and keys and the daily mail are dropped onto the antique desk. All aspects contribute to the impression that function works in complete harmony with beauty (*above*).

*The kitchen* in the circa 1730 home of Andy and Laura Payne of Benchmark Builders, who specialize in antique restoration, mixes old-world style with modern amenities. Andy enlisted Klaff's designer Annette DePaepe for the kitchen's complete renovation. The wood-topped console set next to the Carrara marble-topped table combines the desire to include an extra work sink with the Country French look of mismatching both alignment and materials. Bohemian *lustres* by Schonbek provide European charm and juxtaposition with the stainless steel Wolf range, the Dacor warming drawer and the Fisher-Paykel dishwasher drawers. (*far left*). ❦ The *pièce de résistance* in this kitchen is the stainless steel and brass-trimmed Morice range, well-known throughout the culinary world for its premier cooking capabilities. Bricks immediately adjacent to the range ensure some protection against an accidental kitchen fire. They lend coziness to the space, as do the hand-glazed tiles in the backsplash. The designer's signature use of man-made "stone" adds textural interest and warmth (*above left*). ❦ Handmade, hand-glazed tiles, signed by the artist, reside over a black-enameled professional Viking range. The warm patina of the tiles is set off by ambient lighting from the overhead vent, which is hidden from view underneath the antique beam (*left*).

AN INCONGRUITY IN SURFACE heights is easily seen in this kitchen. The L-shaped island, custom-designed by the homeowner, stands at the industry standard of 36 inches high. The homeowner knew that she wanted to incorporate a marble-topped table for preparations in baking; she intentionally placed one of disparate height directly adjacent to the island. Note how the table also juts out significantly from the edge of the island. This conscious move on the homeowner's part is a distinctly Country French design technique; the French, however, might not necessarily be so conscious of doing so! They might bring in an antique table passed down in their family or picked up at a local market; the worry of it not aligning would not enter into the design decision *(left)*. ❧ The homeowner of this kitchen is a professional baker with her own catering business; she asked the designer to incorporate a marble-topped working area into the cabinetry configuration upon a major kitchen renovation. Here, a piece is constructed between higher cabinets to give the impression that it is a separate piece of furniture. It serves its purpose well: the homeowner uses this distinct part of her kitchen to do preparations for baking *(above)*.

THE CENTER ISLAND in Monique Shay's expansive kitchen has a wonderful provenance. Reclaimed from a shop where it was used as a tool bench, Shay brought it home, scrubbed it clean, redesigned it and added her signature handpainted, hand-rubbed finish. With its 3-inch-thick pine top and lovely shade of blue-green, it complements all of the other design elements in the room and serves as its cornerstone. Because of its massive size, Shay was able to add a sink and still retain a vast expanse of clean work space.

# THE DESIGNER OF THIS *glorious* COUNTRY FRENCH KITCHEN COMMISSIONS HER FAVORITE *SCULPTEUR*

*sur pierre* from the south of France to hand-carve sinks for her clientele stateside. This is one of the finest examples I've seen. Made of Jerusalem Gold marble from Italy, it possesses dominant veins of red throughout. The sink is oversized, thick and perfectly cut. It is, in fact, signed by the artisan. Running your hands across its smooth surface is like touching a stick of soft butter. The copper faucet is from Herbeau (*facing*). ❦ This sink is cut by the same *sculpteur sur pierre* and commissioned by the same designer. Hand-carved by the artisan in the south of France, it is made of native French limestone. Weighing in at two tons, it is deeper and is outfitted with a stainless steel drain. It, too, is signed by the artisan. The wall-mounted faucet is brushed nickel (*above*).

## THIS PROFESSIONAL *baker* AND GOURMET COOK PREFERS TO HAVE EVERYTHING CLOSE AT HAND.

The cutting board, placed next to the white porcelain farmhouse sink and atop the softer, beautiful limestone counters, provides a practical alternative for the chopping requirements of daily food preparations. Note the homeowner's preference for easily accessible pots and pans; they hang next to the industrial range on an overhead rack. Also of interest is her colorful spice shelf, which is within full view and easy access. Bowls rest underneath in the custom-designed cabinet; knives are attached to the side of the stainless broiler on a magnetic strip (*above*). 🌿 When the homeowners purchased their late nineteenth-century chateau-style estate home in the main-line area of Philadelphia, the kitchen had been completely remodeled. A few years later, the couple decided that it no longer fit the needs of their growing family, but they hesitated to do a down-to-the-studs renovation. Instead, they opted to hire artist C. Barry Marron to come alongside and infuse their large kitchen with the *joie de vivre* that it required. Walking through the expansive grounds, the homeowner, a passionate gardener, recorded every single flower growing on the property. This served as inspiration for the artist, who then masterfully handpainted each flower onto a separate cabinet door—including the panels on the Sub-Zero refrigerator/freezer—after the underlying oak was stripped and painted. Light sanding of the artful handpainted design followed, along with an ochre/burnt umber/raw sienna combination glazing to lend depth and an aged quality. Several coats of polyurethane were applied for protection. The result is nothing short of glorious! Note the imported iron chandelier, which continues the floral theme (*right*).

## THE HOMEOWNER OF THIS *newly* RENOVATED KITCHEN PLACED HER SIX-BURNER VIKING

range directly into the wall, hiding much-needed ventilation underneath the antique reclaimed beam from Pennsylvania. She designed the tumbled marble harlequin backsplash, incorporating wonderful copper inlays and outlining it with tiles so that it appears to be a framed work of art. The two stainless steel Wolf wall ovens are both traditional and convection units and are wisely placed adjacent to the range with an appropriate amount of soapstone countertop nestled in between (*left*). ☙ This design—with the six-burner Thermador range and matching double stainless steel wall ovens—incorporates just enough counter space to juggle bowls, baking sheets and utensils used in the preparation of

the family's daily meals. The custom-designed hood, a signature element of this French designer, allows for proper ventilation (*above left*). ☙ These double ovens and industrial-strength stainless steel restaurant-quality range by South Bend were moved by the homeowner from her previous home to her current one as if her family's future depended on it! Massive in scale, the appliance is designed for heavy-duty commercial use. With its built-in broiler, full-sized griddle, six burners, two full-sized ovens, warming lights, exhaust fan and stainless steel hood, it is not designed for the faint of heart. The homeowner, a serious chef, demanded appliances to match her fearless spirit in the kitchen (*above right*).

THIS FABULOUS BLUE-PAINTED *cupboard* WAS BUILT
BY JOE GIUNTZ, A LOCAL MASTER CARPENTER

commissioned by the homeowner. It serves as the family's breakfast bar and appliance center. The center doors open to reveal a coffeemaker and toaster, making breakfast preparations a delightful and easy-to-assemble family experience. These small appliances rest on a sliding wooden tray, which is tucked away when not in use. The space above serves as additional dish storage for those plates not displayed in the lovely black-painted and hand-rubbed plate rack constructed by Giuntz after the homeowner showed him a photo of one she admired in a design magazine. The buttercream lower cabinetry was designed by Rutt Studios and incorporates wicker baskets, which hold onions, potatoes and other nonperishable foodstuffs. Note the variety of cabinetry configurations, panel designs, painted finishes and hardware; this is a decidedly

Country French design approach, one which the homeowner, a professional interior designer and self-described serious Francophile, consciously put into play (*facing*). ❦ The cabinetry in this newly renovated 1930s Pennsylvania stone house was designed by the homeowner and crafted by local master carpenters. Using a wide variety of woods and painted finishes as well as cabinet styles, the pieces were designed with an eye for beauty but with a mind for function. This knotty pine piece by Rutt Studios combines an old-world aesthetic with a modern-day sensibility. The microwave oven is hidden behind the paneled middle section. The sliding pull-out holds spices. The unit was consciously designed to look like a piece of furniture rather than an installed cabinet. The various iron drawer pulls contribute to this wonderful design orientation (*above*).

## CHAPTER THREE

An authentic Country French kitchen is *utilitarian* in nature, for it

serves as the workhorse of the home. Marble tops tables where pastry dough is rolled;

soapstone imbues sinks where vegetables are washed; and unglazed limestone or

earthen terra-cotta supports legs that stand in preparation of each day's meals.

# Expressing Personal Style

Designed by St. Charles of New York, this butcher-block prep table juts out significantly from the L-shaped granite-topped island and adds a distinctly Country French flavor to the room. The generous 3-inch-thick slab of solid maple allows for food prep without worry. The enormous wrought-iron pot rack overhead was crafted by a metal artisan and is attached to a mahogany lightbox.

How does one infuse a kitchen with Country French style? What design elements elicit a Country French ambience? And what, exactly, defines a kitchen as being Country French in nature?

While we traveled throughout the American countryside photographing kitchens and talking with their homeowners and designers, we heard this question more than any other: "What makes a kitchen Country French?" My immediate response of "I know it when I see it" is the typical answer of most people who admire this style of decorating. We know it because we feel it in our bones. But it was never the answer that they were truly seeking. And even though I still believe this to be the intuitive reply to their question, I know that homeowners require a clearer definition of this widely coined stylistic interpretation. Once something is more clearly defined, it usually can be more authentically reproduced.

The truth is, Country French style is decidedly individualistic. None of the kitchens in this book look the same. Some possess a highly decorated style, with custom cabinetry and customized painted finishes enduring a rigorous selection and installation process; others reflect a casual style executed by the homeowner on a strict budget. Some lean toward classic American design, with simple clean lines merely punctuated with Country French accents. Some place a high value on the incorporation of antique accessories and antique furniture pieces in the overall design scheme; others desire brand-new woodwork, fabrics and china for what they consider to be a fresh start or the masterpiece of their newly constructed home. Some homeowners spend months doing the research on their kitchens, as they want a completely authentic room held on the same level as the other completely authentic French rooms in every single living space of their estate homes, or *chateaux*. Others want the kitchen to be the only Country French space in an otherwise traditional American design orientation.

And yet each one of these kitchens possesses elements of Country French style. You need to be able to identify these unique stylistic elements as you go about designing your own new kitchen, remodeling your existing one or gaining insight into simple adjustments and accessorizing.

## COUNTRY FRENCH STYLE DEFINED

Authentic Country French kitchens always use native organic materials. This emphatically defines Country French style. Authentic Country French kitchens look no further than their own town or village in utilizing materials for their homes. They use indigenous stone, indigenous wood and indigenous clay. They know a local craftsman—*compagnon*—and they choose him to produce wares for their living spaces. They choose locally produced *faience* to brighten their shelves and locally produced stemware to hold their wine. Even the humble rooster, locally raised and kin to most natives of the south of France and the long-standing icon evocative of Country French style, takes its place as the official beckoner of each new day!

French country folks use limestone or earthen terracotta from the nearest quarry for their floors; they do not use carpeting—or the dreaded linoleum—as many of us do in America. And while they might choose to accent their tiled floors with handmade rugs, they might just as well prefer to let the sun drench them so as to provide vistas of glistening cleanliness. And they do not keep their tile solely on the floors; thankfully, their practice of using it on backsplashes above ranges has found its way into American kitchens *en masse*. Incorporating tile into walls and around windows has become a distinct element of Country French style both in France and in America.

Authentic Country French kitchens use native soapstone for their sinks; they might use it on their countertops as well, unless, of course, they prefer indigenous limestone or wood. Marble is more commonly found on side tables rather than on long expanses of countertops or on kitchen islands. Indeed, the concept of a center kitchen island is more distinctly American than it is French. An American interpretation of Country French design incorporates a center kitchen island and places a pot rack overhead, which instantly lends both a European flair and a cohesive design element.

Authentic Country French kitchens use wood from native trees for their armoires and cabinetry. In the early seventeenth century, local craftsmen used whatever native woods were plentiful and easily workable. Styles swung from primitive renderings for tables, with straight legs and three or four widths of wood for tops, to more intricately carved pieces following the influence of the Baroque period. In homes across France today, these pieces are found in ample supply and are passed from one generation to the next, prized for both craftsmanship and utility. Armoires, used in the kitchen for storage of linens and china rather than as entertainment centers or clothing wardrobes as we do in the States, remain a staple in authentic Country French kitchens.

## FUNCTION INTERSECTS BEAUTY

An authentic Country French kitchen is utilitarian in nature, for it serves as the workhorse of the home. Marble tops tables where pastry dough is rolled; soapstone imbues sinks where vegetables are washed; and unglazed limestone or earthen terra-cotta supports legs that stand in preparation of each day's meals. Materials serve function and are always put to use as such. They are chosen for durability, for practicality and for accessibility, yet they are always prized for their inherent aesthetic qualities.

Authentic Country French kitchens utilize inherited antiques to hold linens and tableware. A baker's rack purchased inexpensively at a flea market holds a prized place alongside more priceless possessions. Wire racks of this type are especially practical storage options, as they are easily transportable from house to house, are generally lightweight and take up little space. As importantly, the ubiquitous baker's rack allows objects easy access as well as good air flow so that freshly baked goods can cool down.

Other horizontal options, namely porous stone countertops or wooden tables, risk ruin if used for such purposes.

Country French style incorporates an unmatched look: new furnishings mix easily with antiques; chairs come from different sets; china and sterling patterns arrive from multiple lineages. And yet each serves a utilitarian purpose: for practical storage of serving platters or dinnerware; for holding bottles of vinegar and oils; for seating a large family. Pieces are cherished for provenance as well as for utility.

Antique plate racks hold dishes more commonly in authentic Country French kitchens than do over-the-counter cabinets; indeed, the concept of incorporating closed, paneled cupboards is foreign to Provençal kitchen style. Unlike Americans, who prefer clutter to be kept out of sight behind beautiful cabinet doors, the French prefer to have objects *sous la main*. So cutting boards, knives, utensils, pots, pans, countertop appliances, breads, and fruits and vegetables all find their way onto countertops and tabletops.

## APPRECIATION FOR AESTHETICS

Country French folk color their homes with the hues found when looking out their nearest windows: the same greens seen on expansive fields in the horizon weave their way into Provençal fabrics; the yellow of the sun or of bales of hay finds its way onto their walls; blues from the sky accent their *faïence*; and reds from the clay-filled earth color their terracotta floor tiles.

Stockpots, sauté pans and sauce pots are made of copper, as it, more than any other material, heats foods quickly and evenly, and then cools rapidly, making the creation of sauces, glazes and gravies a delightful experience. Lest we forget that France holds the birthright for gastronomical magic, we must understand that, as such, French cooks value the tools of the trade. They desire the best cooking materials, and so cooks of all economic backgrounds in France possess copper cookware; indeed, it is prized throughout generations and becomes part of one's dowry! In authentic Country French kitchens, copper hangs freely from pot racks and is cherished for both its monetary value and for its native beauty.

Country French folk use fabrics from the local mill for their curtains and their tablecloths. Large checks are juxtaposed with *toile de jouy*, and delightfully so. These fabrics are quintessentially Country French. Small-scaled Provençal fabrics bring both color and cheer to kitchens across France, and it is this constant juggling back and forth between seemingly disparate objects and shapes, between formal and informal, between large scale and small that adds to the drama that we adore in the Country French style.

Indeed, beauty is always factored into the French design equation. The French never allow practicality to steal the show; rather, practicality is always *infused* with beauty.

And so open shelving, which is widely implemented in authentic Country French kitchens because of the accessibility of all tools of the trade—mixing bowls and casseroles, coffee cups and juice glasses—are always artfully arranged. Their order, the way items are stacked, inherent patterns and colors will all be taken into consideration in an aesthetically appealing way. For beauty is never forgotten in the interplay of form and function. Armoires might hold antique linens that are used everyday to line tables and to dry dinner plates, yet they will be lovingly rolled or folded so that their beauty is evident to all. The philosophy of function and beauty playing off each other is basic to French culture. Even children are taught to value aesthetics and to view art and beauty with priority.

## CONSENTING TO CHAOS

And yet Americans find many of these ideas unappealing. They view the notion of using open shelving in their kitchens to be impractical at best and downright silly at worst. For we tend to view our kitchens—our renovated ones at least—as "trophy rooms." We invest tens, if not hundreds, of thousands of dollars renovating them whether we cook in them or not! And while we want all the bells and whistles that come with those dollars, we want our spaces to be efficient and streamlined. We want them beautiful, to be sure, but in a different way. We want our kitchens to contain all of the commonly held treasures of well-appointed rooms from our American perspective: custom cabinetry must perfectly align and it must also hide our dinnerware, our stemware, our serving pieces and our groceries. Our refrigerators must be covered in wooden panels to match our expensive custom-crafted cabinetry. Our appliances must be commercial-grade and, as of late, constructed of stainless steel, whether we know how to use them (or clean them!) or not. And our jars of flour and sugar must be hidden behind closed doors, along with our rolling pins, our measuring cups and our mixing bowls.

Not so the Country French cook! He or she prefers to keep these commonly used items displayed in full view and with easy accessibility. The French cook likes to quickly grab a spoon when the pot of stew needs stirring, rather than search frantically in drawers or cabinets in the middle of creating culinary magic. The Country French cook knows how to use her range and cares less than the typical American cook whether or not her range is the *crème de la crème* La Cornue, or whether it is a simple four-burner electric stove.

Perhaps it is our Puritan roots, our parent's experiences during the Great Depression or our American need for efficiency that drives us to these differing design parameters; authentic Provençal design turns a decidedly different corner to be sure. While one approach is not more correct than the other, distinct differences prevail, and you as the homeowner need to determine which approach is more appropriate for you and your family. You need to decide how much efficiency you are willing to gain—or give up—by subscribing to a more authentically Country French design aesthetic and approach.

## A PENCHANT FOR DISPARITY

The Country French kitchen typically possesses a table on which the family eats all of its daily meals and over which wine and conversation flow freely. This table might be a prized family antique, intricately carved and highly valued for its provenance, or a simple, unadorned, locally crafted piece—a *table de ferme*—with little value other than pure sentiment. In rural France, the kitchen and family gathering place—*salle*—is the equivalent of America's family room. Many homes across France do not possess separate dining rooms, so tables and other large pieces of furniture in Country French kitchens typically serve multiple purposes. The kitchen table might be the place where meals are enjoyed . . . and it might also be the area where children do homework and painting projects. The table might serve dinner guests . . . and it might also serve as the place one pays bills. Whatever its varying purposes, as long as the table has good clean lines and solid quality wood and craftsmanship, it will honor the French longing for form and beauty.

Chairs fit nicely around the table, allowing for large gatherings, and might be priceless heirlooms as commonly as *chaises pliantes*, metal slatted folding chairs—French bistro chairs—brought in from the garden. A fully matched set bears no greater enjoyment for daily use than do mismatched ones; the French easily juxtapose disparate objects, placing old next to new, prized next to inexpensive and large scale next to small. It is this give and take, this freely exchanged interplay that brings *joie* to homes across the Provençal countryside.

In seeking to infuse Country French style into your American kitchen, examine your predispositions and leave prejudices at the door. Although you might subscribe to the commonly held American ideal of "a place for everything and everything in its place," remember that we hold no special bragging rights to this *modus operandi*. The French are not sloppy people! Hardly so. Infusing *joie* by incorporating disparate objects and artful confusion to the mix are not mutually exclusive to maintaining order and neatness. The French have figured out how to do both. It is the underlying *approach* to style that separates the two cultures. Approaching design as fun exploration into your personality and your soul, as creative nurturing in your children and in those whom you love, is, by its very nature, authentically Country French. And yet it can be easily implemented by Americans. It is simply a matter of training (or retraining) your eye—and your heart—for looking for *joie* in the everyday moments of life. Exploring the simple things in life with vibrancy and verve. Creativity. Appreciation for beauty and for history. Country French style is accessible to all of us. We just need to seek it and re-create it in the corners—large and small—of our lives.

This homeowner desired very little wall-mounted upper cabinetry, choosing instead custom-designed and crafted armoires throughout her enormous, newly renovated kitchen. This armoire is crafted of knotty pine and possesses glass-paned doors so her extensive collection of everyday dinnerware and crystal could be seen but also kept from accumulating dust balls. Note the different woods used immediately adjacent to each other; the wood on the cabinetry underneath the sink is completely different than the wood used on the armoire, as is the wood used on the center island (*above left*). ❦ Commissioning a master carpenter to craft doors with raised and flat panels, the owner opted for a black-painted finish to add yet another color to her artfully designed room.

The upper cabinet was built around an antique set of leaded glass windows that the owner found while shopping; the woodwork used throughout the entire bar area was designed and built around this single element, giving credence to the notion that antiques can, indeed, be used as the cornerstone of kitchen design. The counter is copper; square nails were hammered in the same way as artisans did in earlier times, adding a wonderfully authentic detail to the space. The handmade copper sink is by Linkasink; the weathered copper faucet is from Herbeau. The knobs are wooden and are painted with the same milk paint that was used throughout the bar cabinetry. The wonderful hinges were found by her carpenter. The backsplash is tumbled travertine marble (*left*).

# THIS IS AN EXAMPLE OF A KITCHEN THAT WAS PART OF A LARGE RENOVATION EMPLOYING

architects, builders and designers. The home added significant square footage in the renovation process, and this room, like others in the home, enjoyed a top-to-bottom overhaul. The result, a large kitchen with a highly polished design orientation, reads "European elegance" and, although it enjoys several design features typical of French country style, it is much more refined by nature. Limestone floors and wood, stone and bronze counters lend a country flair. The white porcelain farmhouse sink is by Herbeau, as are the copper sink in the island and the weathered copper faucets (*above*). ❦ This kitchen is another example of mixing modern amenities into an older home . . . and of evoking a completely different Country French style in the process. The home, a Westchester County, New York, classic French manor house, contains details throughout signifying its provenance. Yet the kitchen was in need of a complete remodel job and, indeed, received wonderful treatment and wise use of space in the process. New custom cabinetry is hand-planed knotty pine; it also conceals the Sub-Zero refrigerator. All of the bells and whistles are included, namely a Wolf stainless steel six-burner range and double ovens, Sharp microwave, Bosch and Miele dishwashers, and Sub-Zero wine cooler. Granite counters and a custom tile backsplash add natural stone and delightfully so. The French bistro stools provide additional seating for this family with young children (*right*).

*This kitchen* similarly evokes
Country French style, and yet it is completely different—
and worked in a different color scheme—than any kitchen
I've ever seen. Designed around the three
clean colors of brown, pink and white,
walking into this room elicits (I would
imagine!) the same response Alice had
when walking into Wonderland: an enormous inner burst of *joie de vivre!* Clean,
slick white surfaces and appliances highlight the room's expansive space. Fanciful
handpainted flourishes abound. Every
corner of the room provides a feast for the
eyes; indeed, the homeowner, a former
stylist, wanted to evoke a "Candy Land"
feel. The large checkerboard floor, painted
in contrasting squares of chocolate brown
and strawberry pink, leads you through
the area, grounding you, thank goodness,
in what could well be a delectable visual
journey of which you might never want
to leave. Look upwards, and you see a
lifelike handpainted mural of a French
*patisserie.* Look sideways and you'll find
handpainted trays bearing roosters. Peek
around the open doorway and you'll find
an entire wall handpainted with words for
every imaginable dessert. Find the nearest countertop and it will be lined with
brown, pink and white candies in perfectly
matched glass canisters. No detail was
overlooked nor was one modern convenience ignored. This Country French
kitchen is like a breath of spring air!

THIS LARGE, DOUBLE, FARMHOUSE *soapstone* SINK IS UNLIKE
ANY I'VE SEEN. CRAFTED OF GREEN SOAPSTONE WITH

a fabulous vein running throughout, the
sink's natural variations make it enormously
satisfying. Its center divider is preferred by
the homeowners, who enjoy washing dishes
together; they love the functionality of using
one sink for washing and another for soaking,
stacking or rinsing. The oil-rubbed bronze faucets by Barber Wilsons are of different heights
and different design, a conscious move by the
homeowner, and one which is not obvious
unless closely studied or viewed head-on. The
counters surrounding the sink are also made of
soapstone and boast a beautiful vein through-

out (*facing*). ❧ The overhead pot rack in this
Country French kitchen holds the homeowner's
prized collection of copper. Made of lovely
oil-rubbed copper, it also holds six electrified
candles, which are covered with Provençal-
style shades. The island is an American interpretation of the long rectangular table set out in
the middle of the room, which is typically found
in kitchens throughout the southern regions
of France. Here, the designer incorporates a
custom-designed piece and tops it with
granite. Note also the hand-carved wooden
brackets (*above*).

THE LIMESTONE FLOOR in this Manhattan home is actually set with new pavers. Designed in a pattern of nine to twelve stones per each large rectangular space, the tiles look as though they have been reclaimed from an antique country home in Provence. Without rugs, the floor maintains the look and feel of sun-glistened cleanliness, the likes of which have earned the French a reputation throughout time.

# THE HANDMADE, *hand-glazed* AND CRACKLED TILES USED ON THE BACKSPLASH IN THIS

wonderful Country French kitchen are from Italy. The homeowner, who played a large role in the design decisions in the renovation—a classically French approach to design—was nervous that the grout used in the tiling process might diminish their patina, color and charm if not done to perfection; he chose to do the grout work himself in the hopes of gaining more control over the final outcome. The result is completely authentic and stunning in its simple beauty (*facing*). ❦ The tiled pattern used on the backsplash was designed by the homeowner, who is a jewelry designer

with a flair for creativity and verve! Deep red and earth-toned tumbled marble tiles are set in a harlequin pattern. Tiny copper inlays fleck the space, adding metallic accents as well as contributing to a totally custom design. The mosaic is outlined with miniature tumbled marble squares that appear to "mat" the underlying artwork; larger brown rope-edged tiles serve to "frame" it. The entire tile art scheme is further surrounded by the same miniature tumbled marble squares, adding cohesiveness to the effect, which is colorful and stunning (*above*).

THIS PAINTED AND *intricately* CARVED ARMOIRE
IS TYPICAL OF THOSE FOUND IN THE FRENCH

Provincial style. Formal and elaborate, with the carved shell detail, scrolled molding and wheat motif, it is right at home in this elegantly designed room. The glass panes allow favorite collections of china to shine through (*facing*). ❦ The homeowner, in her extensive renovation, desired to use hand-crafted armoires for storage rather than wall-mounted upper cabinetry. Through clever design—as well as countless antique shopping trips throughout the eastern Pennsylvania countryside—she successfully achieved a brilliant and uniquely designed room. The Sub-Zero 700 Series refrigerator and freezer are hidden behind red-painted panels of reclaimed barn wood. Four separate freezer drawers are hidden below. The homeowner was particularly vigilant in getting the coloration perfect. The antique armoire adjacent to the hidden Sub-Zero was built in parts: the homeowner discovered three sets of antique doors on one of her jaunts; each had wonderful original paint and coloration as well as metal grating up top. She enlisted the help of her master carpenter, who built an armoire around them, matching panels and paint to the original (*above*).

A WIDE VARIETY OF natural materials are incorporated into this kitchen with striking results. Slate and wood cover the floor; limestone lines all counters; antique reclaimed beams imbue the ceiling with warmly colored wood; porcelain fills the sink; marble tops the pastry table jutting out from the center island; and real wood (no laminate here!) in eight different painted finishes rounds out every available inch of wall space. This kitchen, inspired by the working kitchens the homeowner had seen on her many trips to France, is the result of tedious attention to detail, masterful planning and the desire to use authentic organic materials throughout the room. One could hardly imagine a more glorious room in which to gather *(left)*. ❦ This homeowner needed a piece in her expansive kitchen to display her prized china pieces. This custom-designed beauty takes its place along the outside kitchen wall. The glass panes allow the collection to come through, while the glass protects it from everyday dust, something for which American homeowners are particularly conscious. The inset drawers and doors below hold linens and other necessary kitchen items *(above)*.

SALLE DE BAIN

• PRIVÉ •

# THIS SMALL, *delicately* ARCHED BAKER'S RACK IS USED IN THE HOMEOWNER'S KITCHEN TO HOUSE

favorite cookbooks and a few copper pots and pans. Charming in detail, with scrolled wrought-iron and brass edging, it is narrow and therefore can be easily transported to other areas of the home—or even to the garden—if needed for storage elsewhere. It is ideal here, however, and adds Provençal flavor to this sweet spot in the room (*facing*). ❧ This is an example of a large baker's rack, used in the homeowner's kitchen to house often-used American splatterware by Bybee Pottery and Mary Alice Hadley,

both handmade in Kentucky and signed or stamped by the artist. Enjoying locally produced earthenware, albeit from American potteries, is an authentically Country French practice. The homeowners, with deep roots in Kentucky, wouldn't think of using any other stoneware. Le Creuset enameled casseroles in classic French blue rest on the top shelf; made of sturdy wrought-iron, the rack can easily bear their weight. Various roosters remind the homeowner to begin each new day with energy and *joie* (*above*).

MISMATCHED CHAIRS surround the home-
owner's antique table, and delightfully so! The table holds material
and sentimental value; the chairs do as well but
at an entirely different level. The captain's chair
is a classic ladder-back with a woven rush seat;
the others range from metal garden bistro chairs
to painted wooden chairs, all of different styles
and lines. The kitchen corner holds the family's
collection of handpainted eggs; all were made by
the couple's three children and hold enormous
sentimental—and aesthetic—value. Dangling
delicately, they bring *joie* to the dining area. The
black wrought-iron chandelier adds cohesiveness
to the space. The total aesthetic—including the
nurturing family time spent here—is authentically Country French (*facing*).   The same
homeowner used mismatched oak furniture to
create an enchanting vignette in the far corner
of the room. Placing the narrow shelf above
the oak bureau, she created a wonderful way in
which to display her favorite ceramic and pottery pieces, all of which are easily accessible and
in full view. Note how the wood does not match,
but rather complements, the other wood used
in the cabinetry in the room (*above right*).   The
homeowner enlisted the help of artist Andrea
Hutter to paint the walls of her Manhattan
kitchen to reflect the wonderful terra-cotta
color found throughout Provence. Applying
various finishing effects in order to achieve the
texture and dimension achieved required several
layers of paints and glazes. The result is stunning
and ties the other design elements in the room
together, particularly the handmade and hand-
glazed tiles found on the backsplash (*right*).

# THE PLATE *rack* IN THIS COMPLETELY RENOVATED KITCHEN WAS DESIRED BY THE HOMEOWNER

so that her pretty china collection could not only be easily accessible but also appreciated aesthetically. Of simple but classic design by Annette DePaepe of Klaff's, it adds a distinctly Country French touch (*above*). ❦ This homeowner, who is constantly throwing dinner parties for large crowds, designed her kitchen around double green-enameled 36-inch Viking ranges, allowing her access to eight burners and two griddles. Suspended directly overhead are iron pot racks designed by Taylor & Ng from Berkeley, California. All of her copper pots are immediately accessible; the fact that they bring a wonderful aesthetic to the space is an added visual treat. On either side of the custom mirror, which is framed in cherry and extends to the top of the 12-foot-high ceiling, are custom-made cherry shelves, which hold large stock pots and others too large to hang. Green enamel crocks hold utensils; vinegars, Kosher salt and staples are close at hand as well. The designer built a table and nestled it to the left of the range; on it rests the toaster. The bottom shelf holds non-perishable foods in wicker baskets (*facing*).

Monique Shay's collection of copper pans hangs from a pot rack directly below the enormous range hood. Next to the rack is a small strip holding two more pans; two other pans are simply suspended from hooks to the left of the range. Copper molds hang on the side of her wood-paneled Sub-Zero refrigerator (*left*). 🍴 This oil-cloth table covering was brought back by the homeowner on one of her trips to France. In classic Provençal fabric, the blue and yellow florals evoke Country French style. Who would know that this kitchen is in a small Connecticut town? (*upper right*) 🍴 Meagan Julian's extensive collection of copper pots and pans are used every day and hang easily from the hard-working, industrial-strength custom-made racks above her double Viking ranges. Preferring the patina of heavily used copper, Julian rarely polishes it (*above*).

THIS *homeowner* CONTINUES HER FAVORITE BROWN,
PINK AND WHITE COLOR SCHEME IN THE PANTRY

area. Practical in its utilization of the entire wall for the storage of china, crystal, linens and serving pieces, it also possesses classic beauty. White-painted cabinetry with glass-paned doors defines the quintessential American butler's pantry in old homes across the country. The homeowner added French panache with the insertion of pink-and-white-striped fabric panels, which is an artful approach to hiding the cabinets' contents. Classic hardware adds yet another touch of beauty to a utilitarian space (*above*).  The dining area of this kitchen is infused with warmth

and beauty. Here, the *tableau* is enhanced with a silk custom-made covering, which is accessorized by wonderful fringe and tassels. Chair backs are authenticated with the family monogram, a design element used throughout the home. Polka-dotted china adds intensely satisfying *joie de vivre!* The crystal *lustre* illuminates the space. The framed oil painting and the collection of brown and white transferware further dignify the area as a meaningful place in which to break bread and share laughter and conversation (*facing*).

## CHAPTER FOUR

Infusing *joie de vivre* into your kitchen has less to do with the quality of your cabinetry and more to do with the quality of your conversation. Less to do with the BTUs of your gas range and more to do with the volume of your laughter.

# Infusing Joie de Vivre

This folk art frog is perfectly in line with Country French style decorating. Discovered on an antiquing trip, it holds a treasured spot on the Julians' kitchen wall, underneath their collection of crystal pitchers. It looks like roosters are not the only animals suitable for a morning's wake-up call!

*Joie de vivre* is a widely used expression, heartily embraced by the French and intriguingly examined by cultures around the world. For we earnestly want to figure out how in the world the French seem to enjoy life so much more than do the rest of us! Literally translated, *joie de vivre* means "joy of life." It is the "hearty or carefree enjoyment of life," according to one dictionary; or the "cheerful enjoyment of life," as defined by another. Envisioned by some as an emotion, such as happiness, it is embodied by others as an overriding philosophy for living. It is a commitment to finding joy in everything: in family, in friends, in conversation, in travel, in celebrations—indeed, to finding joy in anything one might do or imagine. It is a decided slant to enveloping oneself in exuberance, regardless of the circumstances in which one finds himself.

You can imagine infusing *joie* into family time. It might involve snuggling on your favorite down-cushioned sofa for a long reading together of your child's current chapter book. Reading the classics with my own children brought me intense joy; I knew I was instilling wonderful stories into their minds and hearts and that pure and honest themes of goodness would remain deeply embedded in their very cores. You can also imagine how you might infuse *joie* into friends and conversation. Lingering dinners in your candlelit Country French kitchen—with steaming vegetables and meats in *soupière en faïence* at your nose and with good drink an arm's length away—are sure to produce hours of joy if food is nourishing and conversation is warm and uplifting.

*Joie de vivre* must encompass everyday moments of our everyday lives. It must not be something that is occasionally sought or temporarily enjoyed. *Joie de vivre* is not meant to be a weekend's excursion into sublime acts of living, fleeting and seldom found. It must be the guiding principle by which one lives his life.

## EMBRACING *JOIE DE VIVRE*

To embrace this philosophy every day, you must come to terms of "from whence cometh your joy?" From your mate? Your children? Your friends? Your faith? Or, for goodness' sake, your La Cornue range? Infusing *joie de vivre* into the most important room in your home requires celebrating life's simplest moments every day with those you come into contact with there. It is so important that it be infused into the kitchen because this is the room in which you derive your bodily nourishment. It is in this room where we ingest life-enriching vegetables and vitamin-loaded fruits. Where we uplift children's spirits. Where we roast chicken and break bread. Where we kiss our spouse before we leave for work in the morning and where we hug best friends when they visit us for Saturday night dinner.

Infusing *joie de vivre* into your kitchen has less to do with the quality of your cabinetry and more to do with the quality of your conversation. Less to do with the BTUs of your gas range and more to do with the volume of your laughter.

*Joie de vivre* is about being joyful with your whole being and with your family and friends. Because we nurture these loved ones in our kitchens, it is the room where it must be most often found. And while I do not want to diminish for even a second the role of other areas of your home where joy is imparted—your entryway where you greets guests, your desk for writing notes of cheer or for addressing birthday cards, or your bathtub for healthy evening sea salt soaks—I do wish to focus on the many small but meaningful ways in which *joie* can be incorporated into the many areas of this most important room.

## OUR NEED FOR *JOIE DE VIVRE*

Infusing *joie* into the home is instinctively desired. We want, as parents and as people, as workers and as lovers, to impart both nurturing *and* aesthetic qualities into those lives in our contact and care. Be they our children, spouses, friends or colleagues, we want people who step across our thresholds to be embraced by our warmth and by things of beauty. Folks who are attracted to the French way of living—and indeed to the Country French style of decorating—intuitively know this. They do not need to be told it or taught it. They know it when they see it; feel it when they are enveloped in it; become intoxicated when they smell it; delight in it visually when they are surrounded by it in every corner.

And so while it might take a little bit of training or readjusting in one's thinking, one can generally find pure "joy of life" by adding touches throughout one's home—and in one's everyday movements through life—in simple yet wonderful and unexpected ways. Be it through a tiny corner sink, lovingly handpainted and carefully outfitted; or a door hinge, painstakingly rescued from the salvage pile; or in homemade cinnamon rolls, heavenly scenting one's downstairs living rooms, those who seek *joie* always find it. Finding joy in life's celebrations—as well as in one's kitchen—does not generally follow a prescriptive. No, finding joy generally comes from allowing it to happen spontaneously—when and where you least expect it. And then to fully embrace it as such.

## IMPARTING *JOIE DE VIVRE*

Every area of your home provides an opportunity for imparting *joie de vivre*. And although *joie* should be sprinkled throughout every room, it is best executed by starting with one room at a time. It requires opening one's eyes and consciously looking for ways to impart it. I found *joie* in kitchens by peeking inside pantries. Surprises of homemade cookies, of private label wines or of extra snacks for the family all made me smile, just thinking of how much fun the family might have devouring these goodies.

I also found *joie* when I poked around homeowner's drawers (with their permission, of course!). Antique silver or wedding china, smartly folded table linens or hand-dipped candles: these small treasures all impart warmth to family and living spaces. They represent tiny acts of kindness and attention to detail that allow others to know that you care about the small things in life as well as the large. For while hunting for a gas range might hold highest priority in the overall scheme or budget of your kitchen, finding Provençal linens for your tabletops might bring you more *joie*. And while fitting doors for your pantry might seem like a bigger deal to both you and your carpenter, stocking those pantry shelves with foods that you know bring both nourishment and pleasure to your family invariably brings more joy to your small children or grandchildren.

Folks who adopt a Country French decorating style for their living spaces invariably appreciate the value of artistry—artistry in painting or in architecture, in scale or in design, in color or in form. And while fine art and design and architecture are prized, to be sure, folk art is highly desirable as well. For it is folk art's qualities of slight imperfection, of irregularities, of oftentimes improper use of scale, form, line or color that drives feelings of *joie de vivre!* Joy is found in discovering untrained talent and treasures unearthed at flea markets. It is found in craftsmanship and in things with generations-old provenance.

Unexpected lighting fixtures always impart *joie*. Bringing exterior fixtures indoors adds the element of surprise to a room. When one sees a formal crystal *lustre* suspended from a tiny ceiling, the juxtaposition alone is sure to bring a smile.

Unusual usage of color also brings *joie*. An apple green pantry is not a commonly found room, after all! Imagine my delight when I walked into the open apple green pantry in a kitchen painted in deep, sun-drenched ochre, which boasted dark green-enameled industrial-strength appliances. The color combination is out of the ordinary. It brings an artistic take to an otherwise mundane living space, infusing *joie de vivre* exactly where it is most needed. Similarly, placing mismatched cabinetry in seemingly mismatched color schemes right next to each other adds the element of surprise and an artistic sensibility that allows the space to speak for its homeowner.

No other room—anywhere—could acquire this look. It is genuine. It is authentic. It is joyful. It is Country French by its very nature.

Bringing the outdoors inside is a decidedly French custom. Thankfully, it is becoming increasingly common stylistically in America as well. Incorporating rustic concrete urns and pots as utilitarian objects for which to hold soap or sponges is a delightful way of infusing *joie* into the kitchen. The homeowner who prefers a galvanized zinc wash basin in which to hold drying dishes to the standard slatted-wood or shiny chrome drying rack shows others that she is willing to take risks in her decorating style—that she will dare to use ordinary objects in extraordinary ways, bringing *joie de vivre* to all who encounter them!

And, of course, bringing nature inside through flowers and animals, and through color and light, always infuses *joie de vivre* into living spaces. Rooms should be filled with evidences of nature. Flowers should find happy homage on horizontal surfaces throughout your home, be they kitchen countertops or bedside tables. Dogs and cats have been our best friends for centuries and circulate the "good feeling" endorphins in the bodies of all who take a few minutes to snuggle with them or to stroke them. Warm earthy colors cannot help but infuse joy into a home; Mother Nature designed the perfect palette. And homes everywhere—as well as those souls living inside—benefit from an abundance of sunlight. Seek to add it in every room possible.

Infusing *joie de vivre* into your life and your home remains your largest challenge, regardless of whether you see yourself as the homeowner or as the kitchen remodeler or as the designer. For infusing *joie de vivre*—joy of life—into daily living each and every day is our largest challenge as human beings. Seek it with all of your senses: with your eyes, in tiny details of artistry; with your ears, in harmonies of classical music; with your nose, in aromas that satisfy your body and soul. Seek to add joy to the daily rhythms of your life and your home. Make it one of your daily missions. I pray that you shall find it.

Bien Vivre~Rire Souvent~Aimer Beaucoup

THE HOMEOWNERS, master builder Don Sturges and his wife, Tina Cobelle-Sturges, who is a highly acclaimed artist in her own right, as well as the daughter of world-renowned artist Charles Cobelle, built their impressive home on what was arguably one of the prettiest remaining estates in Fairfield County, Connecticut. Their home is punctuated with family works. In her distinct style of art, she brings a keen attention to detail. This is especially pronounced in her kitchen, where a light painted treatment was done over the arched window: *Bien Vivre-Rire Souvent-Aimer Beaucoup.* Indeed, "Live Well–Laugh Often–Love Much" should be our life motto. It captures the essence of infusing *joie de vivre* into your kitchen and into those lives in your care. The island's granite is Uba Tuba; the island sink is copper, as is its faucet. Countertops are Creamy Harvest granite with an Ogee edge, beautifully complementing the warm earth tones in this expansive room. The large white porcelain farm sink has a detailed fluted front; the faucet is brushed nickel. The backsplashes throughout are slate.

THIS HOMEOWNER HAS A *delightful* SENSE OF HUMOR; IT IS EVIDENT IN THIS LITTLE CORNER OF

her wonderful Country French kitchen. Antique tins mix comfortably with brand new ones. It is this artful arrangement—the balancing of patterns, colors and shapes in a most charming way—that adds *joie* to her space. The limestone ledge, which serves as a testament to the quality of materials used throughout the room, provides the playful juxtaposition for which the French are well-known (*facing*). ❧ When we photographed this house, I happened to walk towards the dining room, just to take a quick peek. I discovered this tiny powder room and couldn't resist a shot. The *joie* found here was completely unexpected. The homeowner purchased this lovely hand-painted sink as a splurge. Its petite corner design makes it a wonderful addition to this small space. The antique brass

soap dish and towel ring add more flair. Note the gorgeous shade of blue paint the homeowner chose for the wainscoting. Combined with barely pink walls, yellow ochre and buttercream doors, and multicolored tile flooring, it provides joy to all who use the room—or simply pass by it (*above left*). ❧ In this laundry room, directly off the kitchen, the homeowner adds yet more delightful touches. She found the antique farm sink at a roadside antiques shop, and then brought it home and commissioned an artist to handpaint it in a brilliant purple hue with a country farmyard animal motif. The gorgeous wall-mounted faucet sets off the artwork and lends Country French flair. The iron brackets support open shelving, which is used to display the homeowner's collection of vases (*above right*).

Could anything provide a more welcoming note than a silk-topped table filled with beautifully stacked bonbons? In this delightful color scheme, used throughout her kitchen, the homeowner infuses bits of *joie* into every tiny space. China cups are decorated with polka dots; the tablecloth is dotted with them, too. The china cake plates are of the brown, pink and white color scheme and are used with great aesthetic effect (*above left*). ❦ The quintessential symbol of Country French style, the rooster takes center stage on this brown-painted wall. Underneath rests a pink and white striped magazine rack, which holds the homeowner's current stash of design magazines. The silk tassel is evidence of her keen attention to detail; indeed, it is an undeniable factor in her decorating equation (*left*). ❦ The homeowner, who confesses to having a penchant for personal monograms, displays her often-used things in the beautiful mudroom just off the kitchen, leading to the pantry. Having a difficult time imagining any mud shedding onto these glorious floors—or "dirtying" up this space—one can envision the joy that the family finds while walking from kitchen to pantry to retrieve needed food items. The uncommon usage of her favorite three colors is evident in this corner of her home. Storage baskets in pink-painted wicker with beautiful linen liners keep things nicely organized. Her favorite brown transferware plates line the wall leading into the brown-painted pantry. The checkerboard painted floors unify the space (*facing*).

*This homeowner* desired to impart beauty to the area above her range so that each and every time she prepared her family's meals, she would smile.

These handpainted tiles do just that. Classic French cooking themes abound, bringing joy to all who view them. The custom-designed range hood, in knotty pine, adds a beautiful design element to the space. Note the fleur-de-lis door knobs used on these wonderfully carved pantry doors as well as the classic French door pulls *(facing and left)*. ❦ Hand-painted tiles are added to the backsplash area above the range. Delicate in detail, they add a custom design element to what would otherwise be a simple practical space. The pot filler faucet in polished nickel is by Herbeau *(above)*.

113

THE FOYER OFF THIS Country French kitchen offers whimsy and a wonderful infusion of *joie*. How often, after all, does an unadorned mannequin stand ready to greet you? The homeowner possesses a lovely sense of fun with the design of her home. The handpainted mural was a surprise gift from her husband; when she walked home from an out-of-town trip, she entered a room filled with art! Note the scrolled iron brackets at the dining area entry; they are typical of the whimsical treatments received by every inch of this much-loved home (*left*).  In this foyer leading to the kitchen, the homeowner allows her love of the classic Country French red and gold color combination to come alive! The antique bench is covered in a red and gold antique blanket; the sofa in the sitting room is dominated by a Country French geometric pattern in the same color scheme. Note the coordinating Provençal wallpaper and the wonderful fringe trim on the sofa and the lampshade. The handpainted mural, leading you to the kitchen, is the area's masterpiece, punching the space with even more *joie* (*above*).

THIS PANTRY IS *painted* IN A STRIKING APPLE GREEN COLOR.
WHAT A WONDERFUL WAY TO ADD FRESHNESS TO WHAT

could be an otherwise mundane space!
Organization has taken a stronghold: shelves
line up perfectly with the ingredients necessary to feed this large family and to entertain
guests as frequently as do this hostess and
her husband, designer Alexander Julian.
Commonly used items are kept within easy
reach; less-used glassware is stored on the
highest shelves. Serving their private wine
reserve is one of the many ways in which
the family indulges their friends and family
(*facing*). ☞ This homeowner prefers to keep
her colorful collection of Fiestaware close
at hand. Large cereal bowls and mugs stack
neatly on the ledge built for this purpose.
These colors play off brilliantly with the
deep colors of Southern France. The yellow
ochre of the walls and darkly stained wood
used on countertops and on this ledge provide the perfect backdrop (*above*).

*This charming* vignette gives testament to the wonders of bringing the outdoors in, and with a seasonal treatment at that. Decorated during Halloween, the antique French birdcage gets stylized as well. The antique ladder-back chair is a classic French element; the table, which is also an antique, possesses a delightfully warm patina (*left*). ❦ The galvanized zinc basin in which the homeowner dries her freshly washed dishes rests next to the white porcelain sink; it contrasts both stylistically and texturally with the polished faucet by Kohler, one of the homeowner's favorite features of the room. Countertops are butcher-block. All cabinets were handpainted by the homeowner. The outdoors appears to have been brought in: ivy grows in a terra-cotta pot high above the countertop in a garden accessory; galvanized zinc pots house other greenery. This sunny little spot brings cheer to all those fortunate to come close enough for a peek (*facing*).

EVEN A TINY *corner* OF ONE'S KITCHEN CAN BE
BRIGHTENED BY THE USE OF SUN-DRENCHED COLOR.

Yellow ochre on the walls is a common scheme in Country French design; in combination with classic French blue, it is an unbeatable way of infusing *joie de vivre* into your home. When the colors of nature are used in one's home, beauty and harmony result, for the colors found in nature always provide the perfect palette (*facing*). ❦ Desiring to paint existing cabinetry rather than replace it, the homeowner commissioned a local artist to handpaint the flowers onto each cabinet face. The result is not only strikingly beautiful, it is also a clever way to recycle existing elements, saving viable resources along the way. And in the end, the homeowner got a completely custom look, turning a previously dark space into a wonderfully cheerful spot—full of *joie*!—in the house (*above*).

- Milk
- Eggs
- Breads
- Croissants
- Cheese

Bon Appetit

The goal for adding *texture* to your kitchen is to incorporate a wide variety of

seemingly disparate materials. By juxtaposing brick to stone to wood to tile to stainless

steel to terra-cotta to pottery, you will achieve a decidedly Country French style in this

most wonderful room of your home.

# Texture and Tactile Elements

In this charming dining room off the kitchen, the homeowner left the stone walls exposed in order to add desired panache and charm. Stone floors likewise offset the hardwood flooring used in the rest of the house. The delicately scrolled bracket holds purely aesthetic appeal; its textural element cannot be overlooked.

Adding texture to your interior living spaces provides not only a visual feast, it also adds tactile sensuality. Rubbing your hands across a limestone countertop provides the pleasure that can only come from incorporating organic materials into your home. That same sensation cannot be found by rubbing your hands across a countertop made of plastic laminate!

Likewise, exposing yourself and those in your company to the aesthetic delight of antique wood beams, brick walls or hand-planed terra-cotta floor tiles is nothing short of glorious. By utilizing natural materials in our kitchens, we allow our senses to be appropriately indulged.

Whether standing on one's feet all day over the counter, range or marble-topped antique table while baking your daughter's birthday cake, stirring your favorite stew or preparing for your weekend dinner party, by utilizing materials that wear well with the human body, one can more easily withstand the rigors of cooking. And, after all, that is what a kitchen is expressly designed for! But lengthy cooking sessions require inordinate amounts of time standing or walking, and only wooden floors or other natural materials will provide the comfort your body requires. And they provide an enormous visual impact, too. Reclaimed limestone or terra-cotta floor tiles add texture unattainable with any other material.

A wine cellar lined in pebbles will likewise provide cushioning for your legs and feet, and it will add enormous textural impact as well. Because wine cellars often include intense exposures to wood through antique wine casks or open shelving or wicker baskets, opportunities for textural juxtaposition present themselves nearly effortlessly.

## WHY TEXTURE?

The goal for adding texture to your kitchen is to incorporate a wide variety of seemingly disparate materials. By juxtaposing brick to stone to wood to tile to stainless steel to terra-cotta to pottery, you will achieve a decidedly Country French style in this most wonderful room of your home. Cabinets made of wood look fabulous when lined with antique earthenware or pottery. The placement of wood directly next to clay is a warm approach to adding texture to your wall space. And it will give your space a look that will be yours and yours alone. By using these two textures side by side, you will not only achieve the visual aesthetic for which you are striving, you will also achieve a textural dimension and organization not found elsewhere.

Similarly, juxtaposing stone to brick near your cooking surface—a distinctly Country French approach to both aesthetics and safety—will reap numerous textural rewards in this small space. A technique commonly employed in France is to line the area surrounding the range with brick so that if an accidental fire ensues, it will hopefully not spread too quickly nor too far. This practical approach to design is also an aesthetically pleasing one. Few things look more charming than the placement of warm handmade bricks directly adjacent to the industrial-strength, shiny surface offered by stainless steel appliances. Too, when these disparate textures are aligned with organic materials in the countertops, a third dimension, texturally, is introduced with great success.

## ADDING TEXTURE

Perhaps the most common approach to adding texture to kitchen areas is by incorporating tile and stone into the surround of the cooktop. Thankfully, this decidedly Country French stylistic measure has found wide appeal in American kitchens. An enormous variety of materials is available for today's remodelers and designers. As is evidenced by the range of styles found in the cooking areas of the kitchens featured in this book, you can add textural interest by simply adjusting the space over and behind your range. Whether you prefer brick or handglazed and handpainted tiles or simple squares readily available through a building supplier, all help you achieve a dimensional aesthetic unattainable otherwise.

Likewise, if you are drawn to the aesthetic and hardworking nature of stainless steel appliances, you will achieve textural dimension not through the slick surface of the range or the oven or the refrigerator, but rather by the juxtaposition to the natural stone flooring or countertops against or upon which they rest. In addition to these more expensive introductions of texture to your kitchen, the simple placement of a well-used copper sauté pan on the steel grate of your cooktop will instantly add the textural element that you are seeking.

Other wonderful introductions of texture are provided by leaving exterior walls exposed in home renovations. Rather than applying Sheetrock over the stone wall, allow it to remain exposed into the addition or new space. Of course, the same effect results when allowing exterior brick walls to be exposed as well.

Another approach to incorporating texture is by introducing unusual elements into the design of your cabinetry. Stylistic twists such as utilizing chicken wire or turned wooden dowel rods add creative design to otherwise monochromatic wall space. Incorporating natural elements such as wicker adds enormous appeal visually as well as texturally. Not only are wicker "drawers" a practical solution to the storage of onions, potatoes and apples, for example; they also provide yet another interesting design element.

Increasingly common are drawer units with exposed glass, which allow for the visual presentation of commonly used foods such as dried pastas or beans. Again, not only do these clever design elements add visually to the overall appeal of your kitchen, but they also add tremendous texture to the room.

Custom-crafted cabinets can also be outfitted with leaded glass, stained glass, chicken wire or chalkboard door fronts. Additionally, cabinetry can be designed with wooden lattice inserts, allowing for exceptional aesthetic appeal, as well as for practical ventilation. Interesting as these various techniques present themselves texturally, they evoke a Country French sensibility to the decoration of your kitchen.

Another popular design treatment of cabinetry is the hand embossment of exposed wood. Range hoods can be custom-crafted to incorporate this textural—and artistic—element. So, too, can legs of kitchen islands or door surrounds in kitchen pantries. Similarly, corbels with intricate carvings are becoming an increasingly popular way to add textural impact to the kitchen.

## ACCESSORIZING WITH TEXTURE

Home remodelers in particular are paying increased attention to the selection of kitchen hardware, and thankfully so! Glorious oil-rubbed bronze faucets are works of art in and of themselves. The variety of styles and sizes is inspiring and offers homeowners of all budgetary constraints opportunities for wonderful additions to these most-used working areas of the room. Work tops and sinks are arguably the hardest working elements in the entire kitchen and should be chosen with a wide range of considerations in mind. Will teenage boys be using the sink in the island? If so, will they manhandle it? Does the faucet allow you to turn water on and off with a simple push of your elbow? You will not always have two hands free, after all. Do you enjoy—and frequently utilize—the spray feature commonly found on luxury faucets? Does the faucet you most admire require upkeep and maintenance? Do you have the personal inclination—or energy—to put into that?

Other hardware that offers textural impact is that of hinges, drawer pulls and door knobs or handles. Finishes range from oil-rubbed bronze to pewter to blackened steel to antiqued brass. Louis XV–style elongated and exposed hinges provide the ultimate in French style and evoke images of antique cupboards, armoires and cabinets found throughout Provence during the course of the past few centuries.

And do not forget the textural impact that hand-rubbed painted finishes impart to your room. If the hand-rubbing or distressed effect allows the wood grains to show through, the effect is particularly stunning and completely aligned with authentic Country French style.

By staying in tune with the need to impart texture to your kitchen, you should find boundless opportunities for adding this most important design element into your room. Keep both eyes open!

THE KITCHEN OF antiques dealer Carole Winer offers numerous opportunities for textural interest. From the top of the room down, note the exposed wooden beams juxtaposed with the wrought-iron chandelier, as well as the *pots de confit* lining the top of the upper cabinetry. The range hood is lined with tiles, as is the backsplash. Atop the stainless Viking range, a ceramic casserole and copper stock pot add more texture, as do the plates lining the shelves immediately underneath the cabinets. Dried flowers hang from an antique wood rack characterized by wrought-iron rods and hooks; counters are of both wood and tile. More copper is suspended from a rack above an antique butcher's table; lined with chocolate molds, it adds textural punch to the room. Winer edged the island counters, which are tiled, with rough-textured horizontal tiles, giving further textural contrast to the space. A hard-working antique wooden table fits snugly right next to it, injecting the area with authentic Provençal flavor. Note the copper sink and faucet in the island. Finally, the floors mix both hardwood and stone; the forty-five-degree angles of hardwood edging the stone squares ground the room and add immense textural delight.

*This wine* cellar is the perfect example of incorporating textural integrity into a room. An enormous wine barrel is now used as pure ornamentation in this wonderful room. Note the rows of wine bricks lining the adjacent wall. The round wood table and bistro chairs encourage friends to enjoy a glass of wine and stay awhile (*facing*). ❦ Another area of this huge cellar holds an antique metal wine rack. Juxtaposed with the wine barrel and an oversized wicker basket, textural appeal abounds. The exposed stone walls and flowing ivy vines add artistic flair to the space (*above right*). ❦ Exposed stone walls in this three-hundred-year-old space is, admittedly, a wonderful jumping-off point. Pebble floors not only cushion one's feet; they also add textural appeal. The wrought-iron hand railing—artfully crafted with a wine room in mind!—adds whimsy and beauty. Wood beams, joints, shelving and ceiling impart warmth and structural integrity. Wicker baskets hold huge bottles and vines. The bottle drying rack, used in rural France to hold freshly washed bottles before refilling, is a collector's item and adds design interest to the space. Note the wine brick underneath the wood beam; Winer uses these throughout her cellar to hold her large collection (*right*).

# AN EXPOSED ANTIQUE *beam* HIGHLIGHTS THIS SPACE; FROM THERE, THE EYE ROAMS TO THE WONDERFUL

antique *pots de confit* lining the shelf above the six-burner Dacor range. The simple decorative accent of adding eucalyptus stems in various pots unifies the theme, adding a creative spark as well as textural interest. The backsplash behind the range is not tiled at all; it is a clever faux painting commission. The stained doors and drawers are inset into Sheetrock, which was painted to resemble concrete (*facing*). ❦ From this angle, it is easy to see how the homeowner chose to incorporate appliances and storage into her space. Double stainless ovens by Dacor

fit into the wall, close to her stainless Sub-Zero refrigerator/freezer. The microwave oven by GE Profile is tucked away into the wall on the opposite side of the room. Above it, hidden behind a pair of antique walnut doors that the homeowner found while antiquing in France, is her television. The wood, which possesses a beautiful patina, coordinates beautifully with the stained drawers used for storing bowls, platters and other necessary kitchen tools. The wood beams add textural and aesthetic interest to the room (*above*).

The turned leg supporting this center island is another striking example of the textural and architectural interest one can add to a kitchen in order to gain a custom look. Designer Jani Caroli prefers using oak in both her cabinetry and in her custom details; here, it shows up in this wonderful high Country French kitchen with enormous aesthetic appeal. Note the Louis XV hinge on the island cabinet door. Juxtaposed to the terra-cotta floors, the result is stunning (*facing*). ❦ In this kitchen designed by Robert Schwartz and Karen Williams of St. Charles of New York, formal details abound. This corbel is intricately embossed with French style. It complements well the color and the texture found in the limestone floors throughout this impressive room. Note the juxtaposition to the tiled backsplash and the honed Absolute granite range surround (*above left*). ❦ This homeowner opted for a more formal look when working with her designer and architect. The custom-designed turned molding on the pantry doors is one example of the exquisite detail found throughout the spacious room (*above right*). ❦ Noted kitchen designer Siobhan Daggett-Terenzi incorporated many custom details in this completely authentic French chateau. Daggett-Terenzi uses a formal twist with this embossed corbel supporting the center island. The textural contrast with the granite countertop is a lovely touch (*left*).

Jani Caroli, known for her high Country French design orientation, lined this kitchen's Morice stainless and brass-trimmed range with bricks. The backsplash tiles are also stone; both are practical and aesthetically beautiful solutions to preventing accidental cooking fires from spreading too quickly or too far. The wall of manmade "stone" is one of her signature design elements. Its textural addition to the room is undeniable. Note how the simple painted treatment on the walls adds further textural interest (*above*). ❦ From this angle, one can examine all of the interesting textural details of this large, beautifully designed kitchen. The textural wall surrounding the range is striking; the terra-cotta tiles, which possess a wonderful patina, are original to the house and add the perfect color complement as well as additional texture. Turned legs on the center island, interesting detail on the shelving unit above the sink, and lattice work on custom cabinetry all add texture to the room (*right*).

TILES ABOVE THIS RANGE POSSESS A *beautiful* COOKING THEME. THEY ARE FRAMED IN TWO LAYERS OF TILE,

grounding them while adding gravitas to the area. The homeowner chose complementary tiles to highlight the range hood. Note the tiles used to edge the tiled counters (*facing*). ❧ A close-up shot reveals the details of the tiles beautifully. Note also the embossed corbel; the juxtaposition of formal to informal is a common thread running through Country French design (*below left*). ❧ This kitchen is decidedly more formal than most categorized in the Country French genre. Of special interest is the bronze-sheathed backsplash over the six-burner DCS range. The embossed corbels supporting the shelf above the range as well as those on the teak-topped island lend a formal air. The counters immediately adjacent to the range are honed Absolute granite. The flooring is limestone (*below*).

# THIS COMMERCIAL *stainless steel* TRAULSEN REFRIGERATOR AND FREEZER IS THE *PIÈCE DE RÉSISTANCE*

in this French chef's home kitchen. As the owner of Bernard's restaurant, an authentically French five-star restaurant in my own small town, she often entertains large crowds and needs industrial-strength appliances that can withstand heavy usage. Note the custom solid cherry cabinetry encasing the unit. Counters are granite. The flooring is limestone. The juxtaposition of shiny stainless steel and glass next to honed stone and polished wood is particularly beautiful (*facing*). ❧ Once again,

we can see the juxtaposition of stainless steel with solid cherry wood as well as with the tile backsplash and stone flooring. The Viking six-burner range and coordinating hood add industrial-strength functionality to the kitchen; the pot filler faucet is another exceptional and often-used feature. The simple use of copper cookware infuses the space with charm and its much-needed soft patina to break the severity of the steel (*above*).

*The cabinetry* in this kitchen includes wicker baskets in which the homeowners store onions and potatoes and nonperishable foodstuffs. Clean and compact, they are a charming way in which to attractively implement extra storage. They also complement the color of the terra-cotta floor and the handpainted walls. Note the turned pull on the refrigerator; it coordinates without being perfectly matched to the turned dowel rods used on the cabinetry. The chicken wire inserts, combined with the wicker baskets, all lend further textural elements (*facing*). ❧ These cabinets, crafted by Mark Wilkinson for Klaff's but custom painted by hand in order to achieve this fabulous Country French blue, incorporate turned wooden dowel rods for a completely individualized look. Note the hinges and coordinating pulls (*above right*). ❧ The homeowner found these metal baskets while antiquing. She thought they would be a great alternative to ordinary cabinet drawers. Giving them a good scrubbing with a wire brush, she opted to leave them in their natural rusted state. Not wanting to risk losing the patina acquired with age and exposure to the elements, she did not protect them with polyurethane or any other sealant. They serve an everyday useful purpose as well as a creative solution to food storage (*right*).

THIS BLACK *La Cornue* RANGE IS FLANKED
BY GLASS-FACED CABINETS, EACH HOUSING

frequently used foods and spices. In addition to adding visual impact to this side of the kitchen, textural interest is gained as well (*facing*). ❦ The cabinets in this house, which dates to 1760, have leaded-glass fronts. With classic white paint and simple hinges and pulls, they are an attractive, integral part of this delightful American interpretation of a Provençal kitchen (*above*).

*These faucets* by Rohl are authentically
Country French in both style and finish. The central
faucet is shown in a satin nickel finish with a white
porcelain lever. A spray attachment
is to the right. The hot water spout is
shown in a Tuscan finish and is to the
left of the central unit. The contrast of
the faucets and the bronze countertops against the white porcelain farmhouse sink by Herbeau is stunning (*far
left*). This weathered copper faucet
by Herbeau is artfully designed and
adds *joie* to the entire island. Sitting
atop Calcutta Gold marble and juxtaposed with the stainless steel sink, it is
a stunning contrast to the clean fresh
look and lines of marble and steel
(*above left*). This hammered copper
beverage sink and copper faucet with
white porcelain lever by Herbeau is
situated in the beverage nook of this
grand Country French kitchen in
Connecticut. With a Miele espresso
machine and U-Line cooler, the
homeowners have every modern-day
convenience—wrapped in Provençal
style—at their fingertips (*left*).

THE LOUIS XV–STYLE elongated hinges used by designer Jani Caroli are part of her signature style. Hand-rubbed so as to add the desired patina, they look fabulous on the painted oak cabinetry that is her hallmark *(below left)*. ❦ The homeowner found these doors while antiquing and had an entire cabinet built around them. Admiring the original paint, she was persnickety in having the master craftsman duplicate the effect on the rest of the new wood so that it had a totally cohesive look *(below right)*. ❦ This homeowner opted to cover her GE Monogram refrigerator and freezer with chalkboard panels to provide an easy and effective way to communicate simple daily messages to her young children *(facing)*.

- Milk
- Eggs
- Breads
- Croissants
- Cheese

Bon Appetit

The kitchen requires elements of *timeworn* natures, of furniture that has

upheld families across continents, of plates that have held dinner for at least a couple of

different generations.

# Art and Antiques

In the kitchen of antiques dealer Monique Shay, an antique handpainted French spice server rests on the wooden kitchen counter along with an antique grinder and pewter mortar and pestle. Shay hangs glistening copper pans and serving pieces simply on the wall. The vignette, incorporating miscellaneous antiques that hold importance to her and her family, cannot be created by anyone else.

It is no accident that a number of art collectors and antique store owners—and their most loyal customers—wove their homes into the fabric of this book. Indeed, those who most appreciate the role of art and of history, and who incorporate both into the most intimate spaces of their homes, tend to epitomize the feel and style—evoke the *joie de vivre*—that I was seeking.

When renovating our kitchens, we are tempted to impart strictly modern elements and up-to-the-minute conveniences: digital timers on steamer units, microwave-and-convection-oven combinations and built-in cappuccino machines instantly come to mind. These, along with über-sleek stainless steel and perfectly factory-painted cabinetry might represent the latest and the greatest, the fastest and the smartest. But they don't necessarily evoke the style and character for which you originally contracted, nor to which you intuitively gravitate.

The challenge, then, is to impart the warmth summoned by a Provençal sensibility with the practicality sought by possessing a modern sensibility. One of the reasons you are most likely working on a modern update in the kitchen—or the complete renovation of one—is because your current configuration and current appliances no longer work. Refrigerators, on average, have a useful life of less than twenty years. Ovens and ranges, too, do not have infinite lifetimes. So renovations are certainly called for every couple of decades or so. And with the need for renovation comes the need to educate yourself on the latest developments in technology and modern engineering, in terms of how both can be applied to this most important room in your home.

Art collectors, antiques dealers and the folks who frequent these establishments seem to have mastered this challenge, for they have always incorporated art and antiques into their homes. No matter the room or space: art hangs, sculpture rests and decoration prevails. Along the way, they have figured out that areas of the kitchen that generally call for custom cabinetry can be constructed, instead, with centuries-old pieces salvaged from either their families or from the wrecking ball. Old pieces will find new uses. Yes: antique pieces thankfully find their ways into updated kitchens and coexist happily even with those boasting the sleekest fittings—and beautifully so.

## ART AND ANTIQUES AT HOME IN YOUR KITCHEN

As you plan the design of your kitchen spaces, think along the lines of general usage. Will this countertop area serve as the place where you will gather to make the morning coffee? If so, can an antique table or cart be used instead of counter space? If you possess an unusually beautiful collection of china, could you incorporate an antique plate rack next to the sink or dishwasher, rather than custom cabinetry, so as to display your pieces? Do you desire to use your counter space for cutting breads and flowers, meats and vegetables? Could you place an antique butcher's table in the space instead to impart warmth and tactile pleasure along with an appreciation for history?

The clever design usage of inset shelving and cupboards in which to display china, pottery and collectibles is particularly Country French in aesthetics and practicality.

Whether you are designing a new kitchen or are involved in a down-to-the-studs renovation of your existing one, ask your builder to consider laying the Sheetrock so that shelving can be built into the wall; the addition of antique doors with antique hinges will allow for a wonderful journey into both the history of France and of ancestry that needs to be appreciated and respected. Bringing antique cupboards and armoires into your kitchen can only add charm and warmth into this room. Few rooms deserve this more!

If your cabinetry is in good shape or is of sound construction, yet you desire to give it an artistic facelift, consider decorative painting treatments. Whether through painted glazes or handpainted flowers, bringing the woodwork to new life will impart the look you are seeking and at a more reasonable cost than full cabinet replacement.

Handpainted furniture retains its charm for generations. In fact, antique country furniture that has been painted is, with few exceptions, always more valuable over time than antique furniture that has not. Whether the furniture has been painted in an overall color or simply decoratively painted, the charm factor alone is worth adding to your home. Consider using handpainted tables and chairs in your kitchen. Add decorative accessories such as handpainted trays. And handpainting on walls, such as light mural work or the areas over windows or sinks—or even up staircases—is completely surprising in its native charm and is evocative of work done by itinerant painters from centuries ago.

## BUILDING COLLECTIONS

Do not underestimate the value of collections and of art collectibles. It is only by building personal collections of things that you hold valuable—sentimental or material—that your home will take on a decidedly unique look. Giving your home its own stamp does not come quickly or easily; it comes after years of painstaking work, of doing one's homework, of study, research, poking around, and traveling. It takes years for design ideas to percolate. And then, like a good cup of coffee, enjoyed much more when sipped slowly and with friends, it takes time for your evolving eye to carefully edit that which you have come to love.

But acquiring art and antiques and arranging them thoughtfully into your home is a necessary step in infusing it with the warmth, charm—personality!—that every authentically Country French home needs. Begin slowly, if you must, but begin the process, for it is a must.

A particularly Country French collection to build is one of antique *pots de confit*, used decades ago to store fully cooked meat and fowl. A collection of them looks perfectly wonderful in today's homes, and adds the texture, color and warmth that we crave for comfort. Copper pots and pans are collectors' items, too, and remain valuable assets in one's family. French pottery and china are expensive, and are categorized as both art and antiques for their unique place in history. With large antique cupboards chock-full of an assortment, one must consider this to be art in the home.

Consider also the incorporation of antique ironwork into your doors and cabinetry. Pantry doors will hold magical appeal if the contents contained therein are partly exposed; scrolling ironwork allows for partial visibility as well as for partial ventilation. Once again, it represents a design element that possesses artistry and practicality.

## MEMORIES OF THE HEART

The kitchen is the room where we break apart bread for bodily nourishment and where we break down walls for intellectual development, where conversations are started and where heated discussions are continued, where broken hearts are exposed and where healing foods are consumed. The kitchen requires elements of timeworn natures, of furniture that has upheld families across generations and continents, of instruments and tools that have been handled by cooks from different cultures, of plates that have held dinner for at least a couple of different families or generations.

Families, in order to be fully nourished, need to have a sense of the giants who came before them, of grandmothers and grandfathers, aunts and uncles, cousins and neighbors, of significance in one way or another. Using items that have provenance grants historical respect to those fortunate enough to gain exposure to them.

I fondly remember as a small girl sipping homemade chicken soup from antique china bowls, wide rimmed and gracefully decorated in elaborate old-world, European style. My Hungarian grandmother loved nothing more than feeding her grandchildren, cooking us our favorite meals when we visited, setting the table, and sitting with us. It mattered less that the various antique linens and bowls were mismatched; several decades later, it is the memory of warm soup that fills my memories and my soul. I remember laughter and long conversations, and while I do not recall the exact serving pieces or the table linens, I distinctly remember that she always enjoyed using a wide variety of them and that she never hesitated to break them out when we came to visit. Growing up

with antique tables and chairs and china and linens and serving bowls provides comfort and a sense of continuity, that life has moved forward to include you, and that it will move forward even further to include your children and others whom you love.

Bringing into your kitchen those elements that impart these same warm sentimentalities—even years later in the form of distinct and happy memories—is yet another reason to include art and antiques in this room. My grandmother was an antiques lover and a lover of all things beautiful. One of the gifts she left me was an appreciation for all things that impart both history and beauty. With a knack for using my hands to create art. To sit at night—even if in front of the television—and make something wonderful. And to fill up one's home with these pieces, no matter how humble.

I possess a strong desire to leave similarly distinct memories to my own children, to fill up our living spaces with things of sentimental natures, to leave as part of my legacy things that I made with my own two hands. Needlepoint samplers, stitched during each one of my pregnancies, line our walls and bear birth years reminding us of who will get which sampler when I have gone to my heavenly home. Needlepoint belts have been stitched as well. Hand-hooked rugs, made with natural hand-cut wools dyed in vegetable oils, have been made for each child and line the hearth of our own American-style *salle*. Oil portraits of our children hang in our living room.

The giant chandelier in our dining room has a story; so too does our dinnerware, our silverware and our glassware. Life holds stories. And our homes hold lives. Our homes need to convey the stories of those who have filled our lives, including those who have come before us and those who have walked alongside us.

It is my hope that as you move further along the journey of incorporating authentic Country French style into your kitchen—indeed, into the nooks and crannies of your home—that you remember always those for whom you are creating. As you attempt to infuse *joie de vivre* into your living spaces—and into every ounce of energy and breath of life—seek to evoke the spirit of Country French style. Seek to impart the spirit of family, of nurturing, of love.

CAROLE WINER USES AN ANTIQUE *butcher's* TABLE IN
LIEU OF ADDITIONAL COUNTERTOP ALONG THIS

wall of her spacious kitchen. It breaks
the monotony of continuous cabinetry and counters—and the inherent
continuous color scheme—and is a
particularly common technique used
among antique enthusiasts. The sharp
contrast in wood variance, thickness
of the cutting area, color and dimension must be noted. Her collection
of antique copper pots hangs above
on a simple iron rack. An oil painting
of her favorite animal brightens the
entire space. Framed between panels

of simple cotton fabric at the windows, the wall comprises a veritable
art collection in the room (*facing*).

❦ This homeowner incorporates an
antique tea cart for her modern-day
"coffee bar." The combination coffee/
espresso machine is always ready for
use; sugars and spices are easily accessible as well. Her children's origami
is suspended from the wall, further
evidence of the homeowner's desire
to impart *joie* into every corner of her
living spaces (*above*).

THIS PAINTED ANTIQUE armoire is French Canadian in provenance and is an example of the highly sought after pieces from dealer Monique Shay. With strikingly handsome bold blue paint and simply paneled doors, it is a centerpiece of the large kitchen of fashion and home furnishings designer Alexander Julian. The art is by California abstract artist Billy Al Bengston (*facing*). ❧ This nook, created by antiques dealer Monique Shay along one wall of her kitchen, holds prized pieces of antique pottery. Shay painted the backboards of the cabinet in a classic shade of red in an effort to highlight these pieces against what would otherwise be a monochromatic space. This practice of punching an area with color, versus applying tone on tone, is a decidedly Country French design technique (*above right*). ❧ This homeowner desired to decoratively paint her existing cabinets rather than replace them with a more expensive alternative. She commissioned a painter to paint and glaze each one, rubbing darkly pigmented glazes into each recessed area of the panel doors to add depth and intensity. Afterwards, individual flowers were painted onto each panel at the direction of the homeowners. The homeowners also kept the granite countertops and Thermador gas range top and double ovens put into play by the previous owners. They did add the tile backsplash, the Italian iron drawer pulls and knobs, and new hardwood flooring (*below right*).

THIS HANDPAINTED piece of furniture holds prominence in this homeowner's butler's pantry of her expansive kitchen. Not only does it infuse the space with old-world charm, but it also gives the entire section of the room added importance. The placement of the *lustre* above creates an inviting and artful setting; the floral arrangement adds further charm. The custom cabinetry in buttercream holds the owner's collection of crystal and provides additional storage space for frequently used items for entertaining (*facing*).  The homeowner commissioned an artist to handpaint a mural above her range evoking a typical setting if one were to peek inside a French *patisserie*. So decorated cakes and cupcakes top pedestals, and pink boxes tied with brown bows and glass jars filled with candy take center stage. A pink-and-white-striped awning possesses extravagant fringe, and curlicues frame the entire painting. If you didn't know any better, you'd believe you were in Paris! This is just one way in which the homeowner brought art—and loads of *joie!*—into her colorful kitchen (*above right*).  These handpainted stair risers are one of the most charming, artful touches that I saw on my travels for this book. Fewer things would bring me more joy every day than these words and the way in which they stamp this home with love. A handpainted mural lines the right side of the staircase leading to the bedrooms. A red painted gate swings open at the top (*right*).

Fear less, hope more

eat less, chew more

whine less, breathe more

talk less, say more

hate less, love more

and all good things

will be yours.

THIS EIGHTEENTH-CENTURY walnut *vaisselier* from the south of France holds the homeowner's prized collection of antique publicity pitchers. The collection has grown to be so large that pitchers are stacked on top of each other. Instead of looking cluttered, it looks picture-perfect. Plates lean forward on top of each other as well. The homeowner collected these pieces during the years she lived in France as well as on frequent jaunts there. The collection has been carefully edited and contains many valuable pieces. Building collections of things that you love not only adds value to your estate but also stamps your home with your unique personality. The end goal is, after all, to enjoy a home that overflows with your individuality and identity (*above left*). ❦ The homeowner uses antique French canisters and lines them up on her windowsill to ensure prominence. Framed by simple yet colorful window panels of Provençal ochre, the vignette is stunning in its simplicity (*left*). ❦ Using antique items in new and clever ways injects instant creativity into a space. Here, the homeowner utilizes an antique shoe rack, commonly used by laborers when they entered the home after a long workday, to hold cookbooks and other *objets d' art*. The handmade pottery lining the top shelf was in the homeowner's family; they enjoy its provenance every day. The large clock is a reproduction. The carved chair is from the homeowner's grandmother and, sporting a Provençal-printed cushion, enjoys prominence in the hallway (*facing*).

THIS IS YET ANOTHER *example* OF A POT
*DE CONFIT.* HERE, IT IS SEEN IN A
completely different color and shape.
It is indeed quite valuable and has
found new use by holding kitchen
tools (*above*). ❦ This collection of *pots
de confit* lines the wooden ledge atop a
stone wall adjacent to a staircase leading to the main floor. Note the unusual
green color variations (*facing*).

*POTS DE CONFIT* line the shelf built onto the homeowner's range hood. These were used in earlier times in the Basque region of southwestern France to store fully cooked meat or fowl in the winter. The meat was cooked in *cremailleres* over a fire in the hearth until done; it was covered in the rendered fat and the pots were then topped with paper and tied with string. This method preserved the meat throughout the long winter months. These pots are now prized by antique collectors everywhere and are quite expensive. Here, lined up on the wood ledge, they disguise the vent and lighting, which are both hidden underneath. Of various sizes and shapes, the collection is colorful and adds texture and warmth to what could be an otherwise plain spot. The hood has been handpainted and glazed in various shades of rich ochre.

IN HER BUTLER'S *pantry,* THIS HOMEOWNER COMMISSIONED THE ARTIST TO HANDPAINT

every possible French dessert that she could think of. Done to perfection, it is hard to imagine that it was all painted freehand. The floor has received similar treatment. The homeowner chose to use only three colors in her space: milk-chocolate brown, cotton-candy pink and whipped-cream white.

The large glass canister holds jelly beans in these three colors (*facing*). ❧ Antique copper pots add instant charm to a kitchen. Widely available, they look wonderful fully exposed when suspended from an antique overhead rack. An antique clock adds further warmth to the space (*above*).

## A FINAL WORD

This journey began with my desire to renovate my own kitchen. Through the course of writing this book—interviewing designers and builders, visiting countless showrooms and testing the many appliances on the market today, and exploring the wonderful kitchens featured herein—I have begun the renovation process. It is my hope that a future book will show you our results.

Along the way, I met Steve Feldman, founder of Green Demolitions. Green Demolitions is a donation program for Recovery Unlimited, a 501(c)(3) non-profit organization that uses recycled kitchens and other materials to help families on the road to recovery. In support of his vision and his mission, a portion of this book's proceeds will be donated to his organization. Please visit www.greendemolitions.org.

Blessings,
Carolina

# RESOURCES

## KITCHEN DESIGNERS

Benchmark Builders
Andrew Payne
96 Old Mill Rd.
Wilton, CT 06897
203.544.7162
www.remodelct.com

Bilotta
Architects & Designers Building
150 E. 58th St. (between Third
Ave. and Lexington Ave.)
9th floor
New York, NY 10155
212.486.6338
www.bilotta.com

Country Loft Antiques
Carole Winer
557 Main St. South
Woodbury, CT 06798
203.266.4500
www.countryloftantiques.com

Cucina Design
Siobhan Daggett-Terenzi
25 Business Park Dr.
Branford, CT 06405
203.315.6645
www.cucinadesign.com

French Country Living
Jani Caroli
34 E. Putnam Ave.
Greenwich, CT 06831
203.869-9559
www.frenchcountrylivingct.com

Gallery of Kitchens & Baths
Matt Cowan
1027 Post Rd. East
Westport, CT 06880
203.226.7550
www.galleryofkitchens.net

Kitchens by Deane
Alice Hayes, CKD, CBID
1267 E. Main St.
Stamford, CT 06902
203.327.7008
www.kitchensbydeane.com

Klaff's of Danbury
Annette DePaepe,
CKD, CBD, ASID
11 Newtown Rd.
Danbury, CT 06810
203.792.3903
www.klaffs.com

Klaff's of South Norwalk
Nick Geragi, CKD, CBD, ASID
28 Washington St.
South Norwalk, CT 06854
203.866.1603
www.klaffs.com

North Salem Design Group
Richard and Susan Romanski
687 Titicus Rd.
North Salem, NY 10560
914.669.5580

Northeast Cabinet Design, Inc.
77 Danbury Rd.
Ridgefield, CT 06877
203.431.9894
www.northeastcabinetdesign.com

Robert Morris Associates
Robert R. Morris
861 Post Rd.
Darien, CT 06820
203.656.3303

The Rutt Studio on the Main Line
Julie Ann Stoner, ASID, CKD
530 W. Lancaster Ave.
Spread Eagle Village, Ste. 910
Wayne, PA 19087
610.293.1320
www.ruttstudioonthe
   mainline.com

SBD Kitchens, LLC
Sarah A. Blank, CKD
154 Heights Rd.
Darien, CT 06820
203.972.8341
www.sbdkitchens.com

St. Charles of New York
Robert Schwartz
Karen Williams
Architects & Designers Building
150 E. 58th St. (between Third
Ave. and Lexington Ave.)
8th floor
New York, NY 10155
212.838.2812
www.stcharlesofny.com

## CABINETRY
Classic Woodworking, LLC
2155 State St. #4
Hamden, CT 06517
203.495.1548

Kitchens by Deane
*See listing under Kitchen Designers*

Klaff's of Danbury
*See listing under Kitchen Designers*

Klaff's of South Norwalk
*See listing under Kitchen Designers*

Northeast Cabinet Design, Inc.
*See listing under Kitchen Designers*

Paradise Custom Kitchens
3333 Lincoln Hwy. East
Paradise, PA 17562
717.768.7733
www.paradisecustomkitchens.com

RJL Woodwork
Richard Latouf
77 Main St.
Newtown, CT 06470
203.426.7747

The Rutt Studio on the Main Line
*See listing under Kitchen Designers*

## CONTRACTORS, SUBCONTRACTORS & ARCHITECTS
Benchmark Builders
Andrew Payne
*See listing under Kitchen Designers*

Cavendish Grey
Architects and Designers
Building
150 E. 58th St.
New York, NY 10155
212.838.2727
www.cavendishgrey.com

Country Floors, Inc.
15 E. 16th St.
New York, NY 10003
212.627.8300
www.countryfloors.com

D&R Schappach Construction
Rick Schappach
74 N. Mountain Rd.
Brookfield, CT 06804
203.740.8717

Great White Painting, LLC
Charles "Chip" Wilson
202 Ridgebury Rd.
Ridgefield, CT 06877
203.894.9564

Gullans & Brooks Associates,
Inc.
Vincent Falotico,
RA, AIA, NCARB
199 Elm St.
New Canaan, CT 06840
203.966.8440
www.gullansandbrooks.com

Homes of Elegance
Jack Arnold
7310 S. Yale Ave.
Tulsa, OK 74136
800.824.3565
www.homesofelegance.com

MLD Hood Design
1107 Taylorsville Rd.
Washington Crossing, PA 18977
215.493.2427
www.mldhooddesigns.com

New Image Renovations
Brian Egan
2 Tenafly Dr.
New Hyde Park, NY 11040
917.417.9965

Peter A. Cole
75 S. Greeley Ave.
Chappaqua, NY 10514
914.238.6152

Ranney Michaels Architects,
LLC
Sharon Ranney,
RA, AIA, NCARB
6 Sconset Sq.
Westport, CT 06880
203.221.3005
www.ranneymichaels.com

Sturges Brothers Inc.
Donald Sturges
24 Bailey Ave.
Ridgefield, CT 06877
203.438.6298

## INTERIOR DESIGNERS
Alexander and Meagan Julian
323 Florida Hill Rd.
Ridgefield, CT 06877
203.431.3707
www.alexanderjulian.com

Country Loft Antiques
Carole Winer
*See listing under Kitchen Designers*

French Country Living
Jani Caroli
*See listing under Kitchen Designers*

James Rixner, Inc.
James Rixner, ASID
121 Morton St., Ste. #4B
New York, NY 10014
212.206.7439
www.jamesrixner.com

Kent Interiors
Denise Morocco
21 Muller Rd.
Kent, CT 06757
860.927.0123
www.kentinteriors.com

Mari Dolby Interiors
Mari Dolby
880 Uwchlan Ave.
Chester Springs, PA 19425
610.827.7107

Robyn Klein
45 Top of the Ridge
Mamaroneck, NY 10543
914.381.3090

## DECORATIVE ARTISTS & ARTISANS
Designs for the Home
Michele Fugazy
Ridgefield, CT 06877
203.438.0882

Fauxward Decorative Painters
Andrea Hutter
Ridgefield, CT 06877
203.244.5252

Jerry Liotta
65 Kings Hwy.
Westport, CT 06880
203.454.7683

Joyce Danko Design
Joyce Danko
1261 Biafore Ave.
Bethlehem, PA 18071
610.954.0465
www.joycedankodesign.com

Kimberly Petruska Designs
Kimberly Petruska
Bethlehem, PA
610.966.5836
www.kimberlypetruska.com

Lou Chiaia
Norwalk, CT
203.856.7851

Tina Cobelle-Sturges
Ridgefield, CT 06877
203.431.8200
www.tinacobellesturges.com

Wilson Design
Chris Wilson
203.894.1064

## APPLIANCES, SINKS & FAUCETS

Asko Appliances
www.askousa.com

Bosch Appliances
www.boschappliances.com

Fisher-Paykel Appliances
www.fisherpaykel.com

Franke Faucets and Sinks
www.frankeconsumerproducts.
com

Herbeau Fixtures and Sinks
www.herbeau.com

La Cornue Ranges
www.lacornueusa.com

Miele Appliances
www.miele.com

Rohl Fixtures
www.rohlhome.com

Thermador Appliances
www.thermador.com

U-Line Appliances
www.u-line.com

Viking Appliances
www.vikingrange.com

Wolf Appliances
Sub-Zero Refrigerators
and Freezers
www.wolfappliances.com

## ANTIQUES & FURNISHINGS

Ash Hill Designs
Rtes. 113 & 401
Chester Springs, PA 19425
610.827.7107
www.ashhilldesigns.com

Country French Collection
2887 N. Reading Rd.
Adamstown, PA 19501
717.484.0200
www.countryfrenchantiques.com

Country Loft Antiques
Carole Winer
*See listing under Kitchen Designers*

Haritz Barne
801 E. Boston Post Rd.
Mamaroneck, NY 10543
914.835.0495
www.haritzbarne.com

Joseph & Peter's Antiques
111 Lancaster Ave.

Devon, PA 19333
610.254.0600

Monique Shay Antiques
Monique Shay
920 Main St. South
Woodbury, CT 06798
203.263.3186
www.moniqueshayantiques.com

Parc Monceau Country French
Antiques
1375 Post Rd. East
Westport, CT 06880
203.319.0001

Pierre Deux
625 Madison Ave.
New York, NY 10022
212.521.8012
www.pierredeux.com